Barcelona

T0283964

Barcelona has been through some turbulent times: the push for
Catalan independence transformed it into a political battlefield;
mass tourism, at times seemingly uncontrollable, has emptied
the historic centre of its inhabitants, who were also traumatised
by the 2017 terrorist attack on La Rambla, the city's most famous
street; and the pandemic, as elsewhere, dealt a heavy blow to its
health system and an economy more reliant on services than many
other places. As a result, Barcelona has now been overtaken by
the Community of Madrid in terms of GDP, in what is no longer a
virtuous rivalry. For many, the model of growth that transformed
the city for the 1992 Olympic Games has run its course – a victim
of its own success or the inevitable consequence of the model
itself, based as it was on the close relationship between the
private and public sectors. Barcelona has responded by doing
what it does best: trying things out, looking for new solutions
and rethinking its identity. In its quest for urban renewal, the
most recent experiment to take place – which builds upon a long
history of ambitious, revolutionary projects – is the introduction
of superblocks, blocks of streets that have been 'pacified' by the
removal of motor traffic with the objective of improving the
quality of life in what is a particularly dense, noisy and congested
city. Even if every project doesn't always work out – the so-called
'Innovation District', established in the 2000s, is showing signs
of premature ageing – the important thing is to keep trying,
and not just when it comes to urban development: before the
hedonistic reinvention of 1992, Barcelona had a reputation as an
anarchist city, a centre of trade-union struggle and resistance to
the Franco dictatorship. This tradition gave rise to the popular
movement responsible for the election of Ada Colau as mayor;
an activist with a radical programme, she has been able to steer
the city through various crises. And while they have few rivals for
devotion to their language and history and traditions – always
believed to be under threat from real or perceived attacks from
the central government in Madrid – the people of Barcelona are
also committed to experimentation across the board, from music
to literature, cannabis clubs to naturist beaches and, of course,
in football. Upholding the legacy of Johan Cruyff's 'total football',
Barça continues to reinvent itself in its quest to play the beautiful
game even more beautifully, and it has built one of the strongest
sides in the football of the future, the women's competition.

Contents

3

The photographs in this issue are the work of Barcelona-born cinematographer **Marc Gómez del Moral**. He has worked on films, TV series, adverts and music videos, with highlights including the videos he made for the Rolling Stones, Dua Lipa, Elton John, Franz Ferdinand and Scissor Sisters. Recently he worked on Sky's Milan-based drama series *Blocco 181*. Having trained on analogue equipment before moving on to digital, Gómez del Moral decided to bring something different to this edition of *The Passenger*. He took the opportunity to wander through the city in which he grew up, looking around him with a photographer's eye, and shot all the images on film, a medium that gave him time and space for reflection, with a self-assurance and lightness of touch that would not have come with digital equipment.

Some Numbers

'NO MATTER WHERE WE COME FROM ...'

The city's total population by place of birth
Millions of people

- ■ **Barcelona**
- ▨ Elsewhere in Catalonia
- ▦ Elsewhere in Spain
- ☐ Abroad

1.8

1.35

0.9

0.45

0

2000 2005 2010 2015 2021

SOURCE: STATISTICAL INSTITUTE OF CATALONIA

EL CLÁSICO

GDPs of Catalonia and the Community of Madrid as percentages of the Spanish total

Catalonia

20 — 18.19 — 20.01 — 19.30

19.00

15

14.47

10

—Madrid

5 7.82

0 1930   1955   1975   1995   2020
Republic Dictatorship
Civil War   Constitutional monarchy

SOURCE: EL PERIÓDICO

DO YOU SPEAK MY LANGUAGE?

Language preferences of Barcelona residents, 2018

- ■ Always use
- ▨ Use often
- ▦ Use sometimes
- ▨ Use a little
- ☐ Never use

26.5% **Mother tongue**
78.7% **Can speak**

Catalan

Castilian

Other languages

0%   25%   50%   75%   100%

SOURCE: GOVERNMENT OF CATALONIA

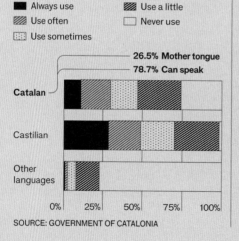

GAUDÍMANIA

Most popular attractions in Barcelona, 2019
Those connected to Antoni Gaudí in bold

FC Barcelona Museum
1,661,156

CosmoCaixa Science Museum
1,002,965

La Pedrera
1,080,519

Parc Güell
3,154,349

Casa Batlló
1,065,222

Picasso Museum
1,072,887

Sagrada Familia
4,717,796

Poble Espanyol Open-Air Museum
1,239,388

El Born Cultural Centre
1,161,755

Aquarium
1,609,373

SOURCE: OBSERVATORY OF TOURISM IN BARCELONA

'MORE THAN A CLUB'

World's top-valued sports clubs, 2022
Billions of $

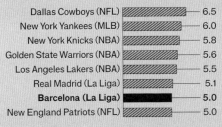

Dallas Cowboys (NFL)	6.5
New York Yankees (MLB)	6.0
New York Knicks (NBA)	5.8
Golden State Warriors (NBA)	5.6
Los Angeles Lakers (NBA)	5.5
Real Madrid (La Liga)	5.1
Barcelona (La Liga)	5.0
New England Patriots (NFL)	5.0

SOURCE: FORBES

EUROPE'S BIGGEST STADIUMS

Seating capacity

Camp Nou
Barcelona
99,354

Wembley
London
90,000

Westfalenstadion
Dortmund
81,359

Bernabéu
Madrid
81,044

Lužniki
Moscow
81,006

Meazza
Milan
80,018

SOURCE: THE STADIUM GUIDE

A PLACE IN THE SUN

Average number of
hours of sunshine in
January in selected
European cities

①

Nice
158

②

Barcelona
149

③

Athens
129

④

Turin
112

⑤

Bucharest
71

SOURCE: STATISTA

BIKE-FRIENDLY
RANKING

13th

in the list of the
world's most bike-
friendly cities,
down from 3rd
place in 2011

SOURCE:
COPENHAGENIZE INDEX

FLIGHT

7,007

the number of
companies that
relocated away
from Catalonia
between the
referendum in
2017 and 2021

SOURCE:
ELECONOMISTA.ES

ANTICLERICAL

Percentage of population who give 7/1,000 of their income
to the Catholic Church, by autonomous community, 2020

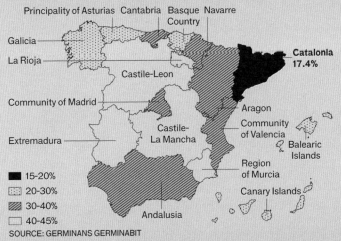

Principality of Asturias Cantabria Basque Navarre
Country

Galicia

La Rioja

Castile-Leon

Community of Madrid

Extremadura

Castile-
La Mancha

Aragon

Community
of Valencia

Balearic
Islands

Region
of Murcia

Canary Islands

Andalusia

**Catalonia
17.4%**

- ■ 15-20%
- ▦ 20-30%
- ▨ 30-40%
- □ 40-45%

SOURCE: GERMINANS GERMINABIT

DECRIMINALISED

Consumption of
cannabis measured
through analysis of
waste water, 2021

Daily mg of THC-COOH
per inhabitant

Barcelona	456
Amsterdam	158
Ljubljana	143
Zagreb	133
Paris	118
Lisbon	102
Innsbruck	98
Prague	91
Cracow	51
Milan	43

SOURCE:
OURWORLDINDATA.ORG

View from the Olympic diving pool in Montjuïc.

The Cycle of '92 and the Olympic Hangover

JORDI AMAT
Translated by Tiago Miller

The 1992 Olympic Games represented an unrepeatable model for growth, and yet the city has stubbornly attempted to replicate it, leaving a trail of failures in its wake and a population losing patience with the high cost of living.

9

Everything was new. The ground floor of the recently constructed building would be the canteen for the athletes who'd be competing in the 1992 Olympic Games that very summer. The building was situated in the heart of a neighbourhood that itself had only recently gone up, built expressly for the occasion and immediately given the name of Vila Olímpica, or Olympic Village. A zone that for centuries had been home to factories, fields and immigrant shanty towns was now being filled with new buildings and new streets named after famous figures from the liberal Catalan tradition who had fought against the Franco dictatorship. From that point on everything acquired new meaning – and from the moment the archer sent his flaming arrow into the cauldron at the Olympic Stadium during the opening ceremony of the games, we Barcelonans changed our relationship with our city. Thanks to our newfound international recognition, we promptly hung a medal around our necks, and it was one of twenty-four-carat pride. This regeneration of an entire identity was inextricably linked to the rediscovery of a coastline that had been forgotten for decades. In fact, the most pertinent and remarkable urban inheritance handed down to us by the socialist founders of the new city (the mayor Pasqual Maragall and the architect Oriol Bohigas) was none other than the opening of the city to the Mediterranean.

A new historical cycle had begun in Barcelona. In order to better reflect on this fact, I decide to return to those very streets. I get off at Bogatell station and begin to walk along streets devoid of people, as is so often the case here. But as I do so, I'm more than aware that I, too, am 'a product of Mayor Maragall' – to borrow a phrase from the architect Maria Sisternas. And, as I walk, I attempt to make sense of what happened in the aftermath of that evening in 1992.

After that miraculous summer, the Olympic Village apartments were put up for sale. Naturally, the athletes' canteen changed function, too. As expected, the building morphed into a cultural phenomenon that was fast becoming established in major urban areas up and down the country: a shopping centre. The one that opened in the Olympic Village was named El Centre de la Vila and was (and still is) the property of a government-owned enterprise. It would be blessed with what the majority of other shopping centres had – a supermarket, shops, bars, restaurants, even a multiplex that screened foreign films in their original languages – but it never took root in the community. The Olympic Village – the transition point

JORDI AMAT is a writer, philologist and journalist. His latest books include the fact-based novel *El Fill del Xofer* and the biography *Vèncer la Por: Vida de Gabriel Ferrater* (both published in Catalan by Edicions 62 and in Spanish by Tusquets). He works for the newspaper *El País*, for which he coordinates the Catalan-language cultural supplement *Quadern*.

Oriol Bohigas – architect, publisher, critic, writer, activist and politician – who died in 2021 at the age of ninety-five, was a classic example of a 20th-century Catalan intellectual and socialist. With his visionary talent he tried to distance himself from the darkness of the Franco regime from the outset, criticising its architectural style and founding Grupo R (R Group – the R standing for renewal and revolution) in 1951. In the 1960s and 1970s he became a key figure in the Gauche Divine, a group of left-wing intellectuals, transforming his apartment into a forum for political debate. His vision revolved around socially responsible architecture, as he wrote in 1964 to an urban-planning committee: 'To be an urbanist today means starting to be a socialist.' Once the Franco regime had relinquished power he immediately began working with the first socialist administrations, and under Barcelona mayor Narcís Serra, he took charge of the city's urban planning, developing a functional strategy with the still-limited budget of a nation in transition. His approach was based on small-scale interventions spread across the city – in line with the slogan 'clean up the centre and monumentalise the periphery' – which focused on the renovation of public spaces: paving, streets, squares, beaches, parks and watercourses. An outspoken polemicist, he railed against the work to complete the Sagrada Família – which he described as an 'anachronistic architectural disgrace', a piece of 'cultural barbarism' that would create a false representation of Gaudí's vision – and in his later years was increasingly in favour of an independent Catalonia, saying, 'It is not that I want to be independent but that I do not wish to be Spanish.'

between the old city and the sea – failed to attract either Barcelonans or tourists, while local residents never managed to create a commercial fabric anywhere near lively or lucrative enough. Notably absent from travel guides, this reality is nowhere better witnessed than when strolling through the aforementioned mall. Today El Centre de la Vila is a void. And, to cap it all, at the back end of 2021 Jordi Mombrú (a journalist at the Catalan newspaper *Ara*) uncovered a disconcerting case of car-park corruption. I can't resist the temptation to see this as a metaphor for the degradation and malaise of an entire neighbourhood, city, moment, country. The end of a cycle.

The company operating the car park in question had stopped paying the owners of the shopping centre. At the same time, this delinquent company was the target of complaints from customers who were unable to take their cars out unless they paid exorbitant fees. Physical confrontations were not uncommon, and neither were incidences of blackmail and hit-and-run. To make things even more darkly complicated, a multimillionaire was unable to take out any of the 350 luxury cars that he had stored on the second floor. Without warning, the company reduced the free customer parking from two hours to one, which only served to create more tension and make the decline of El Centre de la Vila even more acute. The result? Empty shops and a certain disdain by an owner studying the situation from the comfort of an office in Madrid.

The case of the failed shopping centre and its contentious car park seemed to be a revealing example of deep-seated problems: an Olympic-sized hangover from Barcelona '92. And it still isn't cured. Yet, without this founding moment, Barcelona as the illuminating, fascinating city that it is today cannot be understood,

THE PASSENGER   Jordi Amat

The iconic 136-metre Telecommunications Tower built on Montjuïc for the Olympics by the architect Santiago Calatrava.

in the same way that its genesis cannot be comprehended without paying heed to the coincidence in the timing of the Olympics and the start of FC Barcelona's most memorable period. With Johann Cruyff at the helm, the club won its first ever European Cup. Wembley Stadium, London, May 1992: Stoichkov rolls the ball, Bakero traps it, Koeman rockets it into the back of the net. It was an injection of pure self-esteem, and it flowed into the euphoric success of the Olympics. But once the fervour had died down (a joy that had the outrageous rumba of the closing ceremony as its lasting soundtrack), the monument to the moment still loomed high over Bogatell Beach.

The Barcelona of today simply can't be explained without the moment it reinvented itself. But what exactly has it transformed into? It's hard to say. During the first decades of the 20th century the city's international image was closely associated with working-class combativeness and the strength of its anarchist movement. But a civil war involving European powers would have a devastating effect on Spain. Barcelona would be forever remembered as both the setting of a classic work of literature and many tragic events: *Homage to Catalonia* by George Orwell and the conflicts in the Republican rearguard that finally exploded into violence in May 1937 as Stalinism sought to punish Marxist dissidence. With the exception of a few anti-Franco protests during the transition from dictatorship to democracy, the capital city of Catalonia ceased to exist as a

NO MORE BULLFIGHTS

Catalonia banned bullfighting in 2010. The final *corrida* was held in Barcelona's La Monumental arena, to cries of 'Dictatorship' from the twenty thousand spectators there to witness the end of a tradition, while animal-rights protestors brandished placards outside highlighting the cruelty of the custom. Nowadays opinion polls tell us that the majority in Catalonia is opposed to bullfighting, although the ban was invalidated in 2016 by the Constitutional Court in Madrid because the bullfight was deemed to be a manifestation of Spain's intangible cultural heritage. Nothing changed, however, and the events are no longer held. Some supporters of bullfighting believe the ban is about politics rather than animal rights, because the *corrida* is something Spanish, not Catalan. In support of their theory they point out that other violent events involving bulls, but with Catalan roots, still take place: *correbous* are a type of bull run in which the animal is let loose in an arena, sometimes with fireworks attached to its horns, to chase a group of men. The bull might not be killed, but it is subjected to debilitating levels of stress. Animal-rights activists counter this by saying that the campaign has nothing to do with political choices and that they would also like to ban the *correbous*. Meanwhile Barcelona's *plazas de toros* have been repurposed: one became a large shopping centre back in 2009, while La Monumental is used for circus events and musical performances – which might perhaps come as a relief to some traditionalists, as one of the proposed plans for the building was for it to be turned into a mosque financed by capital from Dubai.

Clockwise from top: Plaça dels Voluntaris Olímpics, dedicated to the thirty thousand unnamed volunteers who contributed to the success of the 1992 games. Robert Llimós i Oriol's work was completed in 1997. *El Cap de Barcelona*, by Roy Lichtenstein, is part of the Brushstrokes series and pays tribute to the city and to Gaudí.
One of the apartments in the Olympic Village that have now become private homes.
Collserola Tower, designed by Norman Foster for the Olympics.

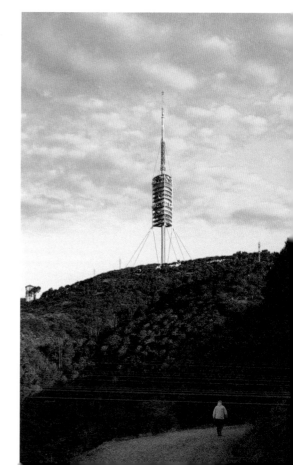

place of interest beyond the general attraction of a 'Spanish' holiday. This inertia was inverted by a multi-level reinvention that had the Olympics as its catalyst thanks to a (perhaps unrepeatable) team of politicians, technicians and experts.

On 17 October 1986, when the International Olympic Committee chose Barcelona to host the 1992 Olympic Games, the organising committee launched the most important urban transformation the city had seen for over seventy-five years. Barcelona shed its skin; the most devastated parts of the old town were cleaned up, and peripheral neighbourhoods were included in the drive to create new hubs outside the city centre. It was a singular case of 'development with a human soul'. In the words of the architect Alessandro Scarnato, reflecting on events in *Barcelona Supermodelo* (2016), it represented the 'transformation of a decaying Mediterranean port into a contemporary metropolis driven by a breed of social democracy non-existent – perhaps even impossible – today'. In *España Fea* ('Ugly Spain', Debate, 2022) Andrés Rubio refers to coastal policies as the paradigm for this type of social-democratic urbanism: 'They built parks, schools and medical centres like the Hospital del Mar, with the most expensive land being saved for public use.' This profound change was implemented with limited levels of backlash. Rubio recalls one controversial act that did take place, namely the city council's decision to demolish the snack bars that peppered the old seafront. These popular bars and eateries – erected without permits and concentrated in the old fishing neighbourhood of Barceloneta – mixed run-down charm with a certain decadent nostalgia. Destroying them was necessary to remove any obstacle between city and sea. Despite isolated complaints, they were flattened,

and Barcelona and the Mediterranean flowed together along one ostentatious avenue.

On 27 February 1991, a year and a half before the opening ceremony, Jaume V. Avoca and Xavier Arjalaguer wrote in the society section of the Catalan daily *La Vanguardia* the following eye-catching headline: 'Just one in eight Olympic hotels meets quotas'. The information was complemented by a piece on the same question: 'Still a city for execs, not tourists'. The report made the alarming claim that two-thirds of those staying in Barcelona hotels were business executives, with tourists making up only 6 per cent. Once all the planned hotels were fully operating, the journalists explained, Barcelona would be one of the European cities with the largest capacity to host business travellers, but the 'Catalan capital will continue to have difficulties attracting mass tourism'. It was a conclusion that the Barcelona Tourist Board had also reached. The news report mentioned that one of the hotels that had indeed reached completion was Hotel Arts in the Olympic Village. The story of this particular hotel is also a metaphor for the Olympic cycle. Naturally, it's located just a stone's throw from El Centre de la Vila.

Its first promoter was the controversial investor and visionary Gooch Ware Travelstead. Son of a building contractor in Baltimore, Maryland, by the mid-1970s Travelstead was embarking on a glittering career as a developer, consultant and financier specialising in real estate. He built skyscrapers in New York and was responsible for the complete remodelling of the old docklands at Canary Wharf in London. When the doors in those two cities closed on him, he turned his gaze towards Barcelona. In 1988 the architect Bruce Graham offered Travelstead and

Eduardo Canet the opportunity to invest in the construction of the Olympic Games' most emblematic hotel. Its location facing the newly rediscovered Mediterranean was unsurpassable. As the journalist Enric Juliana wrote at the time, the hotel was 'private finance's main contribution to the Olympics'. Travelstead's offer allowed him to take possession of the land, but the investor that his associate Canet was charged with finding never materialised, and business relations between the pair gradually deteriorated until they finally severed ties altogether. Eventually Travelstead found the money he needed: the Japanese business Sogo provided the finance, forming a company called Hovisa in the process. The first stone was laid in December 1989, and, according to the developers, just thirteen months later the 'plumbing was in place'. The building is 153.5 metres in height, making it one of the tallest skyscraper in Spain at the time. The same company was also busily erecting a shopping centre designed by Frank Gehry right next to the hotel.

The design by architects Graham and Gehry was modern and elegant, but the operation was an economic disaster. Some of the rooms were ready in time for the Olympics, but the inflated construction costs meant that both Travelstead and Sogo lost a small fortune and more than a few nights' sleep. While the city was still enjoying the fervour of that miraculous summer, the company declared a suspension of payments. First Travelstead backed out and then Sogo.

The auditor put the Japanese company's shares up for sale. Various offers were made. With the auction being held soon after the shock of 9/11, it was a group spearheaded by Deutsche Bank and an American investment company that finally acquired the hotel for €285 million. Just three years later they sold 80 per cent of the property for €280 million. The purchasing consortium contained some of Spain's leading fortunes. However, in 2006 Hovisa was sold again, with the investment fund Banzai purchasing it for €417 million.

But if Hotel Arts is a metaphor, then what for? For the deviation that the city has continued to follow as a result of its mutation. But the change affected both city planning and self-perception. In other words, it was both internal and external. Barcelona was now supping at the top table with other major world cities, not because it was an imposing state capital, or because the money flowing through it made it an economic capital, or because its heritage made it a picture-postcard city (it has Gaudí, but it will never be Florence). Rather it was because the belief that the Catalan capital offered visitors a pleasurable, personal, urban vivacity really took root: a high standard of living thanks to a winning formula that combined Spain, Europe, the Mediterranean, beaches, food, design and culture. Everything one could wish for and, what's more, with *soul* – oh, and southern prices, of course. This would be its role in the cast of world cities

In one of those ironies of fate, the man who set in motion the revitalisation of Barcelona, which had felt neglected under Franco, by awarding it the Olympic Games was someone who had colluded with the dictatorship: Juan Antonio Samaranch. The powerful president of the International Olympic Committee, who hailed originally from Barcelona, occupied a number of posts over his career, in part thanks to the friendship between his wife and Franco's daughter. During the Transition he served as ambassador to Moscow, and, thanks to votes from the Eastern Bloc, he was successfully elected to the top job in the Olympic organisation in 1980. Over the years rumours circulated that Samaranch had been recruited by the KGB and that the Soviets had blackmailed him after discovering his illegal trafficking of works of art. But he remained in office until 2001 and is regarded as the man who, for better or worse, revolutionised the games, contributing to their commercialisation and drawing a line under the controversial rule stipulating that only non-professional athletes could compete. Wider geopolitical events then helped him overcome the tensions and boycotts of the Cold War. It was Samaranch who found a solution to the issues surrounding the break-up of the Soviet Union by allowing the Unified Team of the Commonwealth of Independent States – which brought together all the former Soviet republics with the exception of Estonia, Latvia and Lithuania – to compete collectively at the 1992 Olympics and which went on to top the medals table. But the games went down in history because of another team, the US basketball 'Dream Team', regarded as the strongest of all time thanks to players like Michael Jordan, Larry Bird, Magic Johnson and Scottie Pippen.

during the era of Western globalisation. A destination promising Mediterranean hedonism with style.

But pleasure-seeking requires infrastructure. If from the 1850s Barcelona had been the axis around which a progressively industrialised region revolved, from the 1990s it would become a magnificent city of services. The new city basked in the glow of tourism, for years the industry seeming to provide only exponential growth. Evidence of this can be found in statistics I take verbatim from Ramon Aymerich's book *La Fàbrica de Turistes* ('The Tourist Factory', Pòrtic, 2021): 'In 1990 Barcelona received 1.7 million tourists. In 2019 it was 12 million. In 2000 the number of passengers that passed through El Prat Airport was 19.8 million. In 2019 it was up to 52 million. Between 2003 and 2019 Barcelona multiplied its hotel capacity by three. The year preceding the pandemic it had 78,582 hotel rooms, a figure that rises to 96,609 if we include the greater metropolitan area.' In 2018, for the first time, the number of cruise-ship passengers surpassed three million at the newly adapted port.

Amid the aforementioned transformation in city planning and self-perception, the conditions were being created for yet another change: its development model. While countless other Western industries fell into economic and social decline as a result of offshoring, Barcelona was one step ahead. It was already dangling the lure of the pleasurable urban experience. Everyone wanted to live that experience, and this became *the* new income stream for the new city. The lifestyle it offered was palpable but also fabulous business. Yet another revealing statistic that Aymerich mentions is that, despite being responsible for 70 per cent of visits during the 1980s, by 2017 business accounted for a mere 21 per cent of total stays in the city. To cut a long economic story short, the city's business interests weren't what was being manufactured there. It no longer had anything to do with the trade fairs (up until then one of the bastions of traditional enterprise) constantly coveted by Madrid and other cities. Now Barcelona's line of business was the city itself.

The deindustrialisation of Barcelona and its sphere of influence (as a result of industrial downsizing) posed no hindrance to money flowing in through other sectors. As a result it wasn't necessary to pay any attention to the most significant structural change being solidified in Spain at the time: the accumulation of power in Madrid. Not just political power (which it had always had) but demographic, economic and, above all, media might, meaning that the constituent dynamic of modern Spain, namely fair competition between Madrid and Barcelona, was ripped up. On a political level this change would have enormous consequences (which would drag on until the constitutional crises of 2017 following Catalonia's independence referendum), but it took years to emerge fully. However, Catalonia's GDP remained stable and – theoretically, at least – top of the rankings in Spain. Money flowed in and out. Transactions were constant. Every year more and more tourists came. The new economic elite was dedicated to tourism and real estate – whether they were *productive* industries or not was beside the point – and in that way the Olympic hangover didn't hang quite so heavy. It manifested itself in a more manageable way, like a headache that only requires a bit of quiet.

But an auteur film would soon warn us of what was coming: *En Construcción* ('Under Construction', 2001), directed by José Luís Guerín. On the surface it appears to be a documentary about the razing of a residential block in El Raval, but, amid the scenes of demolition workers, residents' daily lives and visions of urban decay, we soon realise that what is being presented to us is not merely the story of a group of residents but the transformation of an entire neighbourhood (see 'El Raval: Capital of a Country that Doesn't Exist' on page 75). As the director said, 'We were raising awareness that a mutation in the urban landscape also implied a mutation in the human landscape.' Few political criticisms of how the city had shed its skin have been made with such poetic brilliance. The film works as a human chronicling of the real estate sector's colonising of the city in order to exploit the gold mine that Barcelona had become. That same year Julià Guillamon's magnificent book *La Ciutat Interrompuda* ('The Interrupted City') was published, revealing the fissure that was opening between the past and the present, a widening chasm into which an entire identity was falling.

National Institute
of Physical Education
of Catalonia

Olympic Park

Picornell
Swimming Pools

Montjuïc
Telecommunications
Tower

Lluís Companys
Olympic Stadium

Palau
Sant Jordi

MONTJUÏC

Ronda de Dalt

Avinguda Diagonal

Ronda Litoral

THE OLYMPIC SITES

➊ Montjuïc

After the Universal Exhibition of 1929, Montjuïc, where it had been held, was pretty much abandoned. The new Olympic Park on Montjuïc became the main venue for the 1992 games with the renovation of the Olympic Stadium and the Picornell Swimming Pools and the construction of the Palau Sant Jordi multi-purpose arena and the complex for the National Institute of Physical Education of Catalonia. The most iconic architecture was entrusted to Santiago Calatrava, who designed the 136-metre Telecommunications Tower, designed to resemble a torch-bearer. Another tower, designed by Norman Foster, was built on Tibidabo hill.

➋ The Olympic Village

The city reclaimed its waterfront, rehabilitating the run-down areas along the coast. The plan, devised by MBM Arquitectes (Josep Martorell, Oriol Bohigas, David Mackay and Albert Puigdomènech), covered an area of 100 hectares and included the construction of the Olympic Village for the athletes (a total of 1,812 apartments, subsequently

sold off) and a new marina. The most iconic new constructions included the Mapfre Tower and the Peix d'Or, an enormous metal sculpture in the form of a fish by Frank Gehry, while a second skyscraper, the Hotel Arts, was added in 1992–4.

➌ Vall d'Hebron

A project conceived by Eduard Bru converted the neighbourhood to the north-east of the centre into an urban park with secondary sports installations.

➍ Diagonal

In the Avinguda Diagonal area around Camp Nou, the pavements and pedestrianised areas were extended.

OTHER INTERVENTIONS

Port Vell

The 'Old Port', a run-down area of empty warehouses, railway yards and factories, was rebuilt to create a shopping centre, an IMAX cinema and Europe's largest aquarium in a project designed by Jordi Henrich and Olga Tarrasó. It is connected

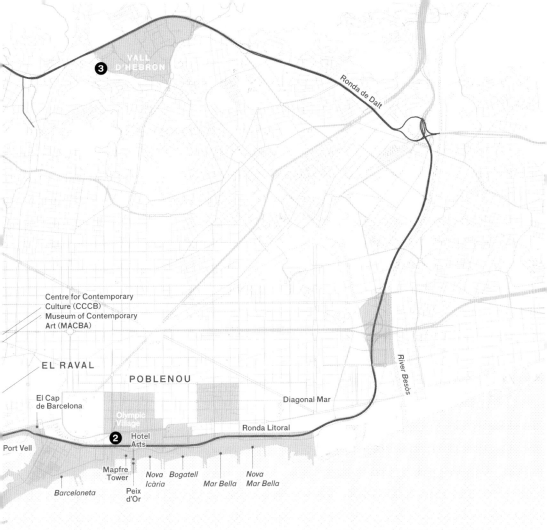

VALL D'HEBRON ❸

Ronda de Dalt

Centre for Contemporary
Culture (CCCB)
Museum of Contemporary
Art (MACBA)

River Besòs

EL RAVAL

POBLENOU

El Cap
de Barcelona

Diagonal Mar

Olympic
Village

Ronda Litoral

Port Vell

Hotel
Arts ❷

Mapfre
Tower

*Nova
Icària*

Bogatell

Mar Bella

*Nova
Mar Bella*

Barceloneta

Peix
d'Or

to La Rambla via a pedestrian walkway with a
swing bridge that allows boats in and out.

El Raval

A project devised by Jaume Artigues and Pere
Cabrera opened up La Rambla del Raval and
transformed the Plaça dels Àngels into a cultural
hub, home to the Centre for Contemporary
Culture (CCCB, inaugurated in 1994) and the
Museum of Contemporary Art (MACBA, 1996).

The beaches

The Coastal Plan regenerated the city's beaches
(San Sebastián, Barceloneta, Nova Icària, Bogatell,
Mar Bella and Nova Mar Bella), cleaning them up
and replenishing them with sand from the seabed.
Purification plants were built on the rivers Besòs
and Llobregat, and the final stretch of the latter
was deviated to the south to expand the port.

The orbital road

To connect the Olympic sites located on opposite
sides of the city, an orbital road was built around
the boundaries of the city (the Ronda de Dalt and
Ronda Litoral) to reduce traffic in the centre. The

investments in transport – which also included the
expansion of tunnels and motorways, the airport
and the metro – were the most expensive of all.

'Barcelona posa't guapa'

The city launched a PR campaign entitled
'Barcelona, make yourself beautiful' aimed at
promoting the renovation of buildings and façades
and the construction of parks and gardens.
The campaign was run in various phases and
ended in 2009 with the redevelopment of around
27,000 buildings, a third of the city's total.

Public art

Installations and artworks by local and international
artists were dotted around the city, including pieces
by Aiko Miyawaki and Rosa Serra (Montjuïc), Antoni
Llena and Auke de Vries (Olympic Village), Susana
Solano and Claes Oldenburg (Vall d'Hebron),
Rebecca Horn, Jannis Kounellis, Mario Merz
and Juan Muñoz (Barceloneta), Jaume Plensa
and James Turrell (El Born). Perhaps the most
representative work was *El Cap de Barcelona*
(*The Head of Barcelona*) by Roy Lichtenstein
in the Plaça de Pau Vila, near the Port Vell.

Nevertheless, the crack was being plastered over by a fashionable brand. Perhaps its best expression is a film that was meant to be called *Midnight in Barcelona* but ended up with the title *Vicki Cristina Barcelona* (see 'An Author Recommends' on page 186). Written and directed by Woody Allen, it was filmed during the summer of 2007 and is the kind of intelligent romantic comedy we've come to expect from the New Yorker. After premiering in September 2008, it earned considerable commercial and critical success: a Golden Globe for best comedy and an Oscar for best supporting actress. The star of the film was Scarlett Johansson, but the Oscar winner was Penélope Cruz. Her role, played to perfection, was (to put it bluntly) simply a twist on Bizet's Carmen – that is, the stereotype of the sensual, passionate Latin woman. The male lead also conformed to the classic model of an irresistible Don Juan, which suited Javier Bardem down to the ground. Both Bardem and Cruz had the perfect profiles for the slight variation being introduced into Woody Allen's work. This variation was the environment: southern European imagery, Mediterranean neighbourhoods and diet, modernist architecture and a diluted representation of the international stereotypes people have of the Spanish. Even the main song from the film's soundtrack reinforced the pleasurable urban vivacity that had catapulted the city into its role as a powerful global tourist magnet. It brought all the required ingredients together to form the perfect postcard

A blood-red mural thirty metres in length painted by Keith Haring in 1989 to raise public awareness of HIV and AIDS.

image. Both the city authorities and the Catalan government put money into the production, having immediately understood that the prestigious association of Woody Allen with Barcelona would make for a magnificent marketing campaign that was 'hip' beyond their wildest dreams and would only further bolster an already highly successful brand.

Could the new Barcelona of '92 have been an influential global city and major decision-maker on the world stage, or was it always just a brand? The most ambitious attempt to revive the social-democratic spirit of '92, through a process of evolution, was nothing short of a farce – and the seafront would also be its stage. From the Olympic Village one can get there by walking in the opposite direction to the Hotel Arts and towards the river Besòs. The principal driving factor in this case was also institutional: the 2004 Universal Forum of Cultures. The festival was based on the open, pleasurable, personal experience that embodied the city's global identity, and leaders wanted to take advantage of it to make Barcelona the place to meditate upon and improve human evolution. Put simply, an utterly insane level of self-indulgence. The Forum was sold as some sort of festival of thought and philosophical reflection but, at the moment of truth, it was nothing but a development operation during the era of a fast-inflating property bubble. From the outset it was clear that it would sink like the proverbial lead balloon, and so it proved.

This monument to failure has served as a fruitful artistic metaphor, grafted on to a revision of capitalism's hopeless drifting after the financial crisis, whether in the stories that make up *Paseos con Mi Madre* ('Walking with My Mother', 2011) by Javier Pérez Andújar, or the criticism contained in Marina Garcés's autobiography *Ciutat Princesa* ('Princess City', 2018), or the art project *Barcelona Vista del Besòs* ('Barcelona as Seen from the Besòs', 2017),

commissioned by Jean-François Chevrier and Jorge Ribalta. Albeit from very different points of view, these are all effective cultural meditations on the erosion of the Myth of '92. Residents accepted the reality that their city was becoming soulless. Luckily, a young Argentine kept their dreams alive every time he had a football at his feet, and for years Leo Messi would allow us to continue believing that we were still living in the best city in the world.

Seen from the outside, that was still the general perception, however, and, to this day, it remains one of the cities where CEOs prefer to live, not to mention being one of the best for a holiday, according to *Telegraph Travel*, the *Telegraph* travel supplement. Yet, despite the city's position in this or that ranking, seen from the inside, unhappiness was everywhere. The awareness of the end of a cycle – of the irreversible erosion of a popular myth that had been defiled by neoliberal ambition – was widespread.

Can the Myth of '92 be resurrected? Right now, the most attractive odds are on trying to push diversification in the development model. A service city, yes, but not *just* a service city. It would mean making Barcelona a metropolis of knowledge, as Miquel Molina explains in his books, in which he correctly identifies nurturing culture (he gives special mention to the activities of the Museum of Contemporary Art and the Centre of Contemporary Culture as key), the start-up economy ecosystem (in and around the port and 22@, the so-called 'Innovation District' – see 'Offices to Let' on page 171) or encouraging high-tech research centres (current notable examples are in biomedicine, photonic sciences and supercomputing). But pursuing a venture that requires the capacity to attract talent and offer them

high-level resources means that the city is in direct competition with dozens of others.

Meanwhile the city's economic motor continues to be the exploitation of the development model that the '92 Olympics made possible, a model still characterised by the integration of private processes into city planning. Does the model have much road left to run? Attempts to update it haven't been in short supply. In 2010 there was the bizarre proposal to host the Winter Olympic Games between Barcelona and the Pyrenees. In October 2012 the then president of the Generalitat, Artur Mas, flew to Moscow to push forward a deal between governments that would accelerate a project that already had private backing: in no more than three years there would be a permanent Hermitage Museum in Barcelona. In fact, negotiations were already under way between

'For many residents, this victory of global capitalism has been nothing but one long hangover.'

the Port Authority, Barcelona city council and investors who, as far as they were concerned, had a deal. The group boasted a Russian construction magnate as its principal partner, and later there was talk of a SICAV investment fund belonging to an Andorran bank entering the deal. Tens of millions of euros. At best, the project might begin to make a profit in the mid-to-long term. If culture is a business then they have a formula for success: the transformation of a global brand into one of the world's most powerful tourist magnets. The project never went ahead. And neither did the creation of a Woody Allen museum.

The result of new planning put in place for the Olympics meant that two large-scale, emblematic projects did indeed go ahead at the seafront area known as Port Vell – and they were emblematic because they ended up highlighting the state of the development model. It was all a bit grim.

One of these projects was, naturally, a mall, the Maremagnum, but, just like El Centre de la Vila, it attracted neither Barcelonans nor tourists. The property has also changed hands, passing from banks to investment groups, but it's never worked as either a commercial hub or an entertainment centre. Nor did the other project, the IMAX. Despite being just a short walk from the city centre, the cinema had to close for lack of customers. On the other hand, another project that did find success was Barcelona Marina. For years it was in the hands of a consortium consisting of a bank and a developer, but the financial crisis forced them to relinquish ownership, and it was acquired by an investment group based in London. The Salamanca Group tabled a proposal to transform the marina so that boats – including some of the most expensive yachts in the world – could moor there. No one questioned the project, nor did the authorities enquire into who was financing it from the shadows at the time. However, the journalist Marc Lamelas did: it was Russian oligarchs using shell corporations registered in tax havens. One such investor who often moored his superyacht there was Alisher Usmanov, who became a target of Western sanctions of Putin's closest allies following the Russian invasion of Ukraine in 2022. But Salamanca sold Barcelona Marina in 2017 to an investment fund from Luxembourg called MIS Nominees and the Qatari QInvest. The latter had also bought one of the last emblematic hotels on the seafront, the W Barcelona.

This is the point at which we must end our tour of the model that was born in Barcelona back in the summer of 1992. For many residents, this victory of global capitalism has been nothing but one long hangover, a grotesque contrast between the pride experienced at the outset of the journey and the horror at what it has led to: evictions, demonstrations against mass tourism and the Olympic Village car-park affair. It also sparked anger and frustration when residents realised that progress wasn't and would never be shared and that many were about to be forced out of the city because of rocketing rents and house prices. 🐦

Is This the World's Most Radical Mayor?

Mayor Ada Colau, first elected in 2015 and for a second term in 2019, has brought social activism into the city's corridors of power. A champion of the fight against mass tourism and a leading figure of the new Spanish and European left of recent times, she is one of that movement's few representatives left in office. Over two terms marked by severe economic and institutional crises, terrorist attacks and a pandemic, has she been able to keep her promise of a new approach to politics that works for the city's people?

DAN HANCOX

Ada Colau, mayor of Barcelona, at the inauguration of the Gabriel García Márquez public library in the Sant Martí district.

It was the early evening of 5 February 2013, and, seated among grave-looking men in suits, a woman named Ada Colau was about to give evidence to a Spanish parliamentary hearing. 'Before saying anything,' she began, 'I'd just like to make one thing clear. I am not an important person. I have never held office or been the president of anything ... The only reason I am here is that I am a momentarily visible face of a citizens' movement.'

Colau was there to discuss the housing crisis that had devastated Spain. Since the financial crisis, 400,000 homes had been foreclosed and a further 3.4 million properties lay empty. In response, Colau had helped to set up a grassroots organisation, the Platform for Mortgage Victims (PAH), which championed the rights of citizens unable to pay their mortgages or threatened with eviction. Founded in 2009, the PAH quickly became a model for other activists, and a nation-wide network of leaderless local groups emerged. Soon people across Spain were joining together to campaign against mortgage lenders, occupy banks and physically block bailiffs from carrying out evictions.

Ten minutes into Colau's forty-minute testimony she broke from the script. Her voice cracking with emotion, she turned her attention to the previous speaker, Javier Rodriguez Pellitero, the deputy general secretary of the Spanish Banking Association. 'This man is a criminal and

should be treated as such. He is not an expert. The representatives of financial institutions have caused this problem; they are the same people who have caused the problem that has ruined the entire economy of this country – and you keep calling them experts.'

When she had finished, the white-haired chair of the parliament's economic committee turned to Colau and asked her to withdraw her 'very serious offences' in slandering Pellitero. She shook her head and quietly declined.

The 'criminal' video became a media sensation, earning Colau condemnation in some quarters and heroine status in others. A poll for the Spanish newspaper *El País* a few weeks later revealed that 90 per cent of the country's population approved of the PAH. The group's work continued. In July 2013 Colau was photo-graphed in Barcelona being dragged away by riot police from a protest against a bank that had refused to negotiate with an evicted family.

Two years later that image went viral, powered by the extraordinary news that the same T-shirted activist had just been elected the new mayor of Barcelona.

On the day of her inauguration Colau addressed supporters of all ages gathered on the cobblestones in Plaça Sant Jaume in Barcelona's old town, thanking them for 'making the impossible possible'. Some waved the tricolour of the Second Spanish Republic, which was declared in the very same square in April 1931; its egalitarian

DAN HANCOX is a British writer and journalist who focuses on music, politics, social exclusion and protest, writing mainly for the *Guardian* and *Observer* but also for *The New York Times*, the *London Review of Books*, *Newsweek*, *VICE*, the *New Statesman* and *Frieze* among others. He is the author of *The Village Against the World* (Verso, 2013), the story of a Spanish town governed as a communist utopia, and *Inner City Pressure: The Story of Grime* (William Collins, 2018), a book on the origins of grime music.

'In July 2013 Colau was photographed in Barcelona being dragged away by riot police from a protest against a bank that had refused to negotiate with an evicted family.'

ideals buried in the rubble of the Civil War five years later.

The date of Colau's victory – 24 May 2015 – was to be, in the words of one spray-painted graffiti slogan, 'a day that will last for years'. Colau had been elected mayor on behalf of Barcelona en Comú (BComú), a new citizens' movement backed by several left-wing parties. She became the city's first ever female mayor, and BComú the first new party to gain power after thirty-five years dominated by the centre-left Socialist Party of Catalonia (PSC) and centre-right Convergence and Union (CiU).

The date was not only significant in Barcelona. BComú was one of several new groups that had defeated the established parties to win power in eight major Spanish cities, including Madrid, Valencia and Zaragoza. These new 'mayors of change' became symbols of hope for what progressives in Spain sometimes call *la nueva politica*. Across Europe, left-wing populist parties and leaders were on the rise.

It became commonplace across the Western world to talk of 'new politics' in response to voter apathy, economic crises, corruption and the decline of established political parties. Sometimes this was a slightly empty label, but in Spain the phrase had a real ring of truth to it. After years of social upheaval following the financial crisis, widespread uprisings against political and business elites transformed the country's political landscape. Just as the Indignados, who occupied Spanish squares in their millions in

the summer of 2011, inspired the global Occupy movement, it was in Spain, too, that this energy was first channelled into political movements capable of contesting elections – specifically, Podemos.

Colau was involved in *la nueva politica* every step of the way, and as mayor of the country's second-biggest city, one of its few figureheads to achieve real political power. Midway through her second term in office she is almost the last woman standing. One decade since she was merely 'a momentarily visible face of a citizens' movement', has she managed to live up to radical promise?

*

When I first met Colau in 2015 she was in the middle of an unusual transition, adapting from grassroots activism to life as an elected politician. Having started out at BComú's spartan office, populated by young people hot-desking on laptops, she was now installed in Barcelona's 14th-century city hall, with its marble columns, stained glass and Miró statues.

Her calendar had been taken over by a succession of official mayoral duties: glad-handing, exchanging gifts and small talk with dignitaries – death by a thousand micro-ceremonies. The demands on her time are especially intense, since it is central to BComú's principles and media strategy that the organisation's figurehead stays on the same level as her supporters, taking public transport and attending neighbourhood BComú meetings where possible.

In the weeks following her victory, Colau signalled what might be new about the new politics with a series of headline-grabbing reforms. 'This is the end of a political class removed from the people,' she said, cutting expense accounts and salaries of elected officials. She announced she would reduce her own pay from €140,000 to €28,600, slashed the budget for her own inauguration ceremony and replaced her predecessor's Audi with a more efficient mayoral minivan. (She was eventually blocked by political opponents from reducing her salary below €100,000 and has stated that she will donate the remaining sum to local groups.) She cut the annual €4 million subsidy to Barcelona's Grand Prix in half, restored school-meal subsidies to the city's poorest children and levied fines worth a total of €60,000 on banks that owned vacant properties. (At the posturing end of the spectrum of political action, she removed a bust of the recent king of Spain, Juan Carlos I, from the city hall's council chamber.) She also spent a night out with a homeless charity, helping to count how many people were sleeping rough in Barcelona (almost nine hundred), met mobile-phone-company workers who were on strike, joined a demonstration against a controversial immigrant detention centre in the city and returned to speak at the very same local assemblies that had brought BComú to power in the first place.

These initial moves encouraged Colau's supporters, but perhaps her most significant challenge – one that has defined her time in office – has been her efforts to tame the more extractive excesses of Barcelona's tourist industry. In its transformation since the 1992 Olympics into the self-styled capital of the Mediterranean and the fourth-most-visited city in Europe,

Barcelona has become a victim of its own success. In the old town, evictions are common – a direct result of rents being driven sky high by tourist apartments – and residents complain that their neighbourhoods have become unliveable in. 'You really can't walk down some streets in the summer,' one local told me, 'as in, you physically can't fit.'

Since coming to power she has frequently been at loggerheads with Airbnb, with city hall ordering the company to remove thousands of unlicensed listings (usually semi-professional tourist operations taking advantage of the platform rather than families letting out a spare room to make some extra cash) – and even fining the company €600,000. The pandemic, of course, did more to overhaul the normal run of things than any politician could dream of – and, unsurprisingly, tourist numbers fell by 70 per cent in 2020. But this was an interregnum that already sees business as usual resuming with gusto: two years on from the first lockdowns of spring that year, the Barri Gòtic, the centre of the old city, is heaving back into life with its usual mingled air of ancient cobbled streets and boozed-up young tourists.

The scale of the city's tourism problem – and how recent a problem it is – is made clear by a few simple figures: in 1990 Barcelona had 1.7 million visitors making overnight stays, only a little more than the population of the city; by 2019 the number has risen to twelve million. In the intervening three decades infrastructure and accommodation were, of course, substantially improved and expanded – pavements widened, signage increased, tour buses rerouted – but the incompatibility is a fundamental one. Barcelona is a relatively small city. It is not London, Paris or New York. Major attractions such

Activists from the Sindicat
d'Habitatge celebrate blocking
an eviction in the old town.

as the Sagrada Familia and Parc Güell are located in the middle of residential neighbourhoods, not surrounded by the open space they need to accommodate millions of visitors.

As tourism has exploded, radically reshaping the city, the question of who Barcelona is ultimately for has become increasingly insistent. 'Any city that sacrifices itself on the altar of mass tourism,' Colau has said, 'will be abandoned by its people when they can no longer afford the cost of housing, food and basic everyday necessities.' Everyone is proud of Barcelona's international reputation, Colau told me, but at what cost? 'There's a sense that Barcelona could risk losing its soul. We need to seek a fair balance between the best version of globalisation and keeping the character, identity and life

of the city. This is what makes it attractive – it is not a monumental city, and it is not a world capital like Paris – its main feature is precisely its life, its plurality, its Mediterranean diversity. We want visitors to get to know the real Barcelona,' she said, 'not a "Barcelona theme park" full of McDonald's and souvenirs, without any real identity.' The change in Barcelona's old town since the millennium is very noticeable. The area is no longer dominated by locally owned restaurants, decked with laminated pictures of sangria and tortillas, or little shops selling matador costumes and Gaudí tea towels. Now its narrow, cobbled streets are watched over by American Apparel, Starbucks, H&M, Disney and Foot Locker. Every now and then, as you stand in the Barri Gòtic and wonder whether the locals who refer to Barcelona as a 'tourist theme park' are being hyperbolic, a bike tour – if you're particularly unlucky, a Segway tour – will spin around a tight corner, and you will have to jump to avoid being body-slammed into an oversized paella dish.

*

While visitors come for the Gaudí mosaics, al fresco drinking and tapas, there is another side to Barcelona's culture – a history of barricades, pitched battles with police and deeply held local neighbourhood identities – that long pre-dates the rise of the tourist industry. In the early 20th century this rebellious side of the city earned Barcelona the epithet *la Rosa de Foc* (the Rose of Fire). It was there that the radical trade union, the CNT, was founded; by 1919 it had more than 250,000 members in Barcelona alone. That same year, a forty-four-day general strike held in the city secured for Spain the world's first national law on an eight-hour working day.

Colau is not shy about expressing her respect for this heritage. She was born in 1974, in the twilight months of Franco's dictatorship, only a few hours after the execution of the prominent Catalan anarchist Salvador Puig Antich – an event that Colau has described as formative. One of her first acts as mayor was to lay a wreath in honour of the anniversary of the execution of Catalan anarchist and educationalist Francesc Ferrer i Guàrdia. It was, she said, thanks to the legacy of figures such as him that she, as an 'activist, rebel and Catalan', could become mayor of the city.

Colau grew up in Barcelona's Guinardó neighbourhood, playing in the streets with her three sisters and other local children – the idealised Mediterranean upbringing where public space is everyone's living room. She grew up in a politicised household and participated in her first protests, against the first Gulf War, at the age of fifteen. She went on to study philosophy at the University of Barcelona and never considered becoming a politician. Later

The origins of the nickname for anarchist Barcelona, *la Rosa de Foc*, go back to 1909 and the unrest surrounding what came to be known as the *Setmana Tràgica*, Tragic Week, between late July and early August of that year. Tragic because of the death toll of more than a hundred people but also because of the political aftermath. The trigger was the call-up of the Spanish army's Catalan reserves, mainly workers who were their families' only sources of income, to fight in the War of Melilla, a colonial conflict in Morocco. The only way to avoid conscription was to pay a huge sum of money or to finance the war through the purchase of weapons. For the working class it was impossible to evade, leading to a series of strikes that the central government attempted to put down by sending the army into the city. The effect was quite the opposite, however, and tensions increased. Trade unionists and anarchists refused to accept the repression, and the protest degenerated into a violent clash during which large numbers of religious buildings were burned down; contemporary photographs show the smoke rising up from the city's roofs. When the regular army overcame the resistance and the unrest began to calm, scapegoats were sought, in spite of the horrified international reaction to the government's violence. Among them was Francesc Ferrer i Guàrdia, an internationally renowned anarchist teacher – between 1901 and 1906 he had run the Escuela Moderna, an experimental mixed school for boys and girls run on secular, rational and anti-clerical lines – who was tried and summarily executed.

she studied theatre for a year. When she was twenty-seven she even appeared in a short-lived sitcom about three sisters called *Dos + Una* – she was the *una*, the eldest of twins.

It was at the turn of the millennium, as the post-cold-war radical left began to coalesce around a series of anti-globalisation protests in the US and Europe, that Colau became more actively involved in politics. She recalls speaking on the telephone to friends in Genoa during the 2001 anti-G8 protests, after a police raid had left sixty-three protesters hospitalised. It is this period, she believes, that laid the groundwork for Spain's new wave of left-wing politics. 'I got involved in 2001 with anti-globalisation movements, against the war in Iraq and the World Bank and global warming,' she told me. 'For hundreds of thousands of people this was the beginning of their involvement with politics, and I still see the influence of this period at work today.'

Colau spent the first years of the new millennium embroiled in activism, protesting and campaigning against wars, poor housing and gentrification. While working for the PAH, she developed her distinctive style of speech, which rests on a sincere, if carefully crafted, populism. She has said that she wants to 'feminise' politics, focusing city hall messaging on issues such as domestic and sexual violence, renaming streets after prominent women and issuing a four-year Gender Justice Plan. But it is also about an approach to politics that seeks open and inclusive debate from the grass roots up rather than conflict and macho rhetoric. It is hard to imagine her saying, as the Podemos leader Pablo Iglesias did at Podemos's founding conference in 2014, that 'Heaven is not taken by consensus – it is taken by assault.' Instead, in speeches and interviews Colau returns again and again to a few central themes: human rights and democracy, participation, inclusion, justice. When I used the word 'radical' at one point, she challenged it with, 'But what is radical? We are in a strange situation where defending democracy and human rights becomes radical.'

A key part of Colau's appeal is that, unlike many politicians, she is not afraid to show emotion. The famous 2013 parliamentary hearing was by no means the only time she has cried or been close to tears on camera. At rallies she uses the whole stage, gesticulating and speaking passionately about the city's most marginalised residents – women and children and pensioners and migrants and the unemployed – only letting herself uncoil when it is over and the BComú supporters are on their feet.

In person she is the same, speaking quickly and seriously, not seeming to pause for breath – then, when the message is delivered, she relaxes, often breaking out in laughter. When I met her on BComú's symbolic hundredth day in power, it was the middle of the Mercè, Barcelona's week-long autumn cultural festival. That week it genuinely felt as though the doors of city hall had been thrown open to the people: normally protected by security guards, the courtyard inside was thronged with festival performers and their families in traditional Catalan folk costumes of red shirts and white trousers; there were piles of rucksacks on the floor, excited children darting about and a baby being changed on an ancient oak bench.

From the moment of her election victory, Colau had echoed the Zapatistas – the revolutionary indigenous group in Chiapas, Mexico – by promising to 'govern by obeying the people', and that night she delivered a speech of studied humility.

Barcelona's main religious festival, La Mercè, which is held in late September and dedicated to the city's patron saint, Our Lady of Mercy, has ancient and miraculous origins: according to tradition, the Madonna appeared on 24 September 1218 to the king of Aragon and the saints Peter Nolasco and Raymond of Penyafort. In 1687 the city decided to make her its patroness following a plague of locusts. When the pope finally approved Barcelona's decision in 1868 the festivities began. The first major festival was held in 1902, since when it has continued through changes of regime and under Franco's dictatorship, adapting to the requirements of whoever was in power – at times intended as a festival of the people rather than a religious event and at other times a conservative, Catholic celebration. Since Franco's death, the democratic and Catalan nature of the festival has dominated: the streets of Barcelona host a series of traditional performances, with dances such as the *sardana* from Girona and the human towers (*castells*) of Tarragona. The events are free, open to the entire population and spread across the different neighbourhoods: alongside the folk dances and puppet processions with firework displays, two festivals are held, one a music festival and the other devoted to the circus arts as well as a race and activities for children. The festivities open with a ceremony in which a speaker directly addresses the city in a speech known as the *pregó*: the website for the event proudly lists all the *pregons* given since 1995 to present an evolving urban pantheon that includes writers, actors and chefs as well as high-profile politicians who have fought for the rights of Barcelona's people.

'Never trust in our virtue or our ability to represent you completely,' she told her supporters. 'Throw us out if we don't do what we said we'd do ... but be conscious that we can't do everything on day one.' It was a response to the paradox at the heart of Spain's new left-wing politics, which depends upon a small number of charismatic leaders. In Barcelona, for instance, this remarkable victory against the established parties by a crowdfunded citizens' platform, formed only eleven months before the election, was built around the appeal of the one woman whose face was on all the posters.

In one of her most high-profile speeches of that first election campaign, at a rally in September 2014, Colau addressed the grey areas in Spain's new populism. 'They will ask us, "Who are you?" Let's not be so arrogant as to say we're "everyone". But we are the people on the street. We're normal people. We're simple people, who talk to our neighbours each day, who, unlike professional politicians, use public transport every day, work in precarious jobs every day and who see how things are every day.' Colau still lives in a modest flat near the Sagrada Familia with her

An employee of the SAD home-care service demonstrates
outside city hall dressed as Ada Colau in her activist guise.

Is This the World's Most Radical Mayor?

In 2010 the owner of the last shipyard that carried out repairs on Barcelona's merchant fleet ceased operations in line with the city's intention to transform its old docks into a fashionable luxury marina where wealthy people from around the world could moor their yachts. This was an initiative that faced opposition from local people, who were concerned that their rents would go up and, more generally, that the neighbourhood would face an indiscriminate tourist invasion. But the protests were in vain, and the controversial project to transform Port Vell, the Old Port, was approved in 2012. As a result, a big slice of public space was privatised and handed over to companies whose main interest was not just to accommodate the huge vessels owned by their paying customers but also to guarantee their peace and privacy by closing the area off and denying local people access. So the view at Port Vell began to be dominated by multi-deck superyachts, which visited not just for their owners to enjoy what the city had to offer but, above all, so that the necessary repairs could be made to their vessels, which became a speciality of the shipyards of Barceloneta. Since the pandemic, which made those who were already rich even richer, yachts and repairs to them have constituted a growth market. And while the luxurious marina might now seem less crowded than in pre-pandemic days, one reason is that the owner intends to reduce the number of moorings, partly to avoid completely obstructing the locals' view of the sea but also in order to specialise in private vessels of more than sixty metres in length, which are becoming increasingly common.

husband Adrià Alemany – with whom she wrote two books about the housing crisis – and her son Lucas. With Gaudí's gargantuan basilica at its heart, and three million visitors a year filling the pavements of an otherwise quiet, residential neighbourhood, it is an area that exemplifies Barcelona's identity crisis.

*

As Colau has found out, the problem with being the people's champion is that not all the people want the same things. In one part of Barcelona's old town, tensions over tourist excess very quickly spilled over into outright hostility. Tucked away from the sea, Barceloneta's narrow streets are lined with tall blocks of flats displaying the barrio's blue-and-yellow flag with a crest featuring a lighthouse and a boat. They are often accompanied by another popular flag, bearing the stencilled Catalan slogan *'Cap pis turistic'* (No tourist flats).

For centuries Barceloneta was a traditional working-class fishing district, until the beach on its perimeter underwent extensive regeneration for the 1992 Olympics. The area is now lined with expensive surf shops, rickshaw drivers, sellers of tourist tat and beach volleyballs. Locals complain that the cost of living has shot up and the hordes of tourists often make for bad neighbours.

Tourist misbehaviour peaked in Barceloneta one Friday morning in August 2014, when three exuberant young Italian men spent several hours wandering around the area naked. Photographs of the streaking holidaymakers quickly circulated on social media, and a series of anti-tourist protests followed. When I visited in 2015 the area was plastered with posters put up by city hall, asking in several languages 'Do you know if you're in an illegal tourist apartment?' Another in the same series

'Cruise passengers who are unlikely to stay overnight in the city or even spend much money at all in their few hours on land were compared to "plagues of locusts".'

instructed 'Don't use the street as a toilet.' By spring 2022 those posters were gone, but stickers reading 'Tourists go home – you are destroying our neighbourhood' were still visible on lamp-posts around Barceloneta, as residents waited to see just how much post-pandemic tourism would surge back again. In the Port Vell Marina just next to the neighbourhood more than half of the berths normally occupied by fancy yachts still lay vacant.

Colau's stated priority has been to move Barcelona away from what she considers 'massified tourism', the kind that offers no concession to sustainability, strategic planning or input from the public. 'Until now all we have had were private initiatives doing what they wanted,' Colau told me. 'This has led to a model that is out of control.' She added, 'We suffered the same short-sighted model here with the real-estate bubble. We are trying to prevent the same mistakes happening again with tourism.'

In 2017 Colau got her controversial landmark bill through a fractious city hall, against great opposition from the tourism industry: banning any new hotels in the city centre and restricting them across the whole city, in an attempt to relieve pressure on the overburdened old town. In 2021 they launched Check Barcelona, a free app for tourists that provides real-time information on how overcrowded particular attractions or areas are in the hope of distributing them more evenly across the city. Many of these initiatives have come from Ada Colau's new tourism council, which features input from ordinary Barcelonans as well as the

industry. Another of her main targets, the cruise-ship industry, remains relatively untouched. Despite promising crackdowns in 2015 and on her re-election in 2019, numbers have been steady, the pandemic aside. Cruise passengers who are unlikely to stay overnight in the city or even spend much money at all in their few hours on land were compared to 'plagues of locusts' by Colau's ally, former councillor Gala Pin.

On the other side of the old town from Barceloneta lies the Raval, another area with a long history of poverty and strident working-class solidarity. One afternoon, I attended a community discussion event here, which took place on ground where a factory once stood. The empty plot was due to have a luxury hotel built on it – instead, the site was occupied by local activist groups who had turned it into a social space covered in graffiti art decrying police brutality and city branding of the 'I ♥ Barcelona' variety. A man named Manel Aisa took the mic to explain that he grew up on this very street in the 1950s, where his dad ran a bar populated by duckers and divers, radicals and sex workers. He explained that the week before he had been walking through the Raval when a group of young German tourists approached him and asked in faltering Spanish, 'Is this a good area to invest in property?' He managed a laugh, recalling the cheek of the question. 'I told them where to go – away.'

But the difficult truth is that for many Barcelonans – not just a wealthy elite of cruise-ship owners, hoteliers and landlords – the tourist economy has been a source of salvation. 'For the majority

A friendly welcome ...

of people sharing their home, it's about making ends meet,' Ricardo Ramos, spokesman for the Barcelona Association of Neighbours and Hosts, explained over lunch near Sagrada Familia. 'We have pensioners who are trying to pay the mortgage or the rent and live on €400 a month – and that's impossible in Barcelona. Some of these people would be on the streets within two months without that extra income.' Ramos's organisation, which was founded in 2015, is supported by Airbnb – but even if it appears to be more 'AstroTurf' than genuine grass-roots, the ambivalent attitude most ordinary Barcelonans hold towards tourism, given so many work in the industry, is very real.

For supporters of Ada Colau and BComú both inside and outside city hall, the years since she was first elected have provided a series of unforeseeable, world-historic distractions and obstacles beyond anything they could have imagined back in 2015. They certainly haven't had an easy time of it. After coming to power in the wake of a global financial and housing crisis, they were then met with the Catalan nationalist wave, 2017's unauthorised referendum and the unprecedented scenes of violence, politically motivated arrests and prison sentences not just of politicians but of cultural figures – made harder by the fact that BComú did not have a declared pro- or anti-independence stance. While it suited chauvinistic bourgeois nationalist parties in both Catalonia and Madrid to keep ramping up the tensions, it had the precise opposite effect for Colau – polarising, alienating and distracting from their city-specific mission. And then there was the 2017 terrorist attack on the city's most famous – and tourist-heavy – thoroughfare, La Rambla, which killed thirteen people, and all that before you even get to the epochal disruption of the pandemic.

'Imagine if we'd had this same opportunity but in a much quieter decade, like the 1990s,' laughed one close ally of Colau, somewhat wearily. 'I wasn't naive when we began, but I was still surprised to find that the people lined up against our project, the people trying to stop us changing things for the better have been more powerful than I ever imagined. They really, really do not want us to succeed.' 'They' amount to a wide range of opponents – from the right-wing Catalan and city press to the Spanish state in Madrid (including – in fact, especially – the governing centre-left Spanish Socialist Workers' Party, the PSOE, who need the populist lodestar to their left to fail, as Podemos have done), to the Catalan independentists, to the representatives of global capital in the city, such as major international hotel chains or cruise-ship owners. 'On the other hand, thank God it was us in power to deal with these crises – what would a right-wing nationalist city hall have done after the terrorist attack instead of reiterating that we are a multicultural, peaceful city where refugees are welcome? Or imagine if the city was run by a party that didn't steer such a careful, neutral line on Catalan independence during 2017 and 2018, when everyone else was pouring petrol on the flames.'

*

Heading up a minority government following both the 2015 and 2019 elections, Colau and BComú have required support from other parties to get new legislation passed. Indeed, their vote share fell from 25 per cent to 20 per cent at the most recent election. The threat that BComú's enemies posed to stable governance was clear from the outset: even before the mayoral inauguration, Jean Delort, the political representative for the Barcelona police, resigned in protest at the election of Colau. 'For them, there are no decent police,' said one police spokesman. 'We're all torturers.'

BComú has encountered substantial opposition in the council chamber from established parties keen to block its more radical reforms and expose its inexperience. The centre-left PSC leader Jaume Collboni has described Colau's anti-tourism measures as 'indiscriminate', accusing her of ideological purism and 'profound ignorance of the terrain' in 'a complex city like Barcelona'. He proposed that the novices in BComú would benefit from his party's governing experience and that only a co-governing pact with the PSC would stabilise the 'extreme weakness' of Colau's administration.

Prior to her first election she had ruled out just such a pact with the PSC – whom she called one of the 'parties of the regime' and, as such, 'part of the problem, not the solution' – but has been forced to rule with their support ever since. For some activists this has been a compromise too far, but for most it has just been an unsurprising if unwelcome bump along the road on the long march from the social movements into the institutions.

But these challenges raise a bigger question for BComú supporters and activists as well as those even more tainted by the stains of power and compromise, such as Podemos: was it all worth the effort? Might they just have been better off lobbying for change from outside their various parliaments? 'Everyone in BComú is now pretty burned out,' one activist told me in 2022, as she took time out following the challenges of the pandemic. 'The problem is, you can't base your politics solely on being the new challenge to the establishment, because you can't be new for ever. Eventually you

Ada Colau meets her voters.

THE PASSENGER Dan Hancox

'The problem is, you can't base your politics solely on being the new challenge to the establishment, because you can't be new for ever. Eventually you become the state.'

become the state. But I'm still so proud of what we've achieved and are achieving.' She points to successes like the traffic-restricting superblocks that have seen families picnicking and children playing in once-polluted streets (see 'Superblock 503' on page 57), and the €150 million Neighbourhood Plan, which uses detailed demographic data to prioritise new investment in the districts with the biggest social problems and poverty.

For some experienced observers, taking activist politics into the institutions of power was always going to be a challenge. Oriol Nel·lo is professor of urban geography at the Autonomous University of Barcelona and a former PSC representative in the Catalan regional parliament, but he has backed Colau and BComú. Grassroots activists should not think of city hall 'as a fortress', he told me over coffee in a cloistered square in the Raval. 'It's better to think of it as a very complex arena in which you can manage to conquer certain positions – knowing that these institutions are more likely, a lot of the time, to give way to other pressures, coming from the economic sector or from business. But that doesn't mean you can't do anything within the institutions,' he smiled. 'You can change plenty of things.'

It is quite something to look around at the other bright hopes for left-wing populism in the West that emerged in the mid-2010s and realise that she now stands almost alone. Manuela Carmena, Colau's ostensible sister-in-arms, the left-wing mayor of Madrid elected in 2015, greatly disappointed her supporters and then lost the 2019 election. Pablo Iglesias, founding leader of Podemos, has left politics as the party's poll numbers continue to dwindle. The idea that Syriza would be a radical force in Greek politics feels like ancient history. Jeremy Corbyn and Bernie Sanders eventually conceded defeat. Jean-Luc Melenchon failed to make the final round of the 2022 French presidential election. But Colau is still there, after navigating a bewildering array of obstacles – some of them expected, but many once-in-a-lifetime events – still governing and still promising more radical changes.

There is a sense among her supporters that Colau's experience fighting for housing reform, occupying banks and blocking evictions with the PAH has given her the confidence and perseverance to keep going. The PAH was, she told me, 'a collective made up of the poorest people in Spain, people who lost everything – not just their homes or their money but their hopes for the future'. With nothing left to lose, they got organised, formed close bonds, supported new friends, joined in civil disobedience together, fought improbable odds – and they won. 'It's an experience I will never forget in my entire life,' Colau said, 'because it taught me the most valuable lesson I have ever learned, which is that we will be whatever we want to be. To have a society that is more just truly depends on us and on whether we get involved or not.' 🐾

The Art
of Observing
Bridges
from Below

Escalators with a view in the Can Zam
neighbourhood.

To see the world from a different perspective is the goal of a somewhat unusual *flâneur*, whose wanderings we follow along the twenty-four stops of Line 9 of the Barcelona Metro, which, once completed, will be one of the longest individual metro lines in Europe. Far from the same old tourist itineraries, our wanderer discovers something more about himself and the city.

LAURA FERRERO
Translated by Simon Deefholts

43

There is no need to go into all the details, much less explain why someone out for a wander should arrive one sunny Friday in April, the 15th to be precise, at ◈ **Can Zam**, the final stop on the northern branch of Line 9 (L9) of the Barcelona Metro. When he gets outside, he is overwhelmed by the sensation that he is at the edge of the city, or, more accurately, at the start of another city (although it will take a while to understand this). To describe his situation, some would use that overworked adjective: lost. But that word has two different meanings. On the one hand, losing things is all to do with the disappearance of what is known, but to get lost is also associated with the appearance of the unknown.

In *Berlin Childhood Around 1900*, the philosopher Walter Benjamin affirmed that in order to really get to know a city you have to get lost in it, actually lost. The passage reads: 'It is of little importance not to know one's way around a city. Getting lost in a city, on the other hand, like getting lost in a forest, is a skill that has to be learned.'

All of us walkers pass through the same places again and again, and our footsteps trace geometrical shapes that wear down those places, whose horizons we diminish through the habit of routine.

And this walker, this traveller, this *flâneur* who emerges from the metro at Can Zam, is now aware of all this.

As we said, there is no need to go into all the details, because now, if someone were to ask the walker why he is there, he would simply offer the best of all replies: 'Why not?'

AN ORANGE LINE ... DISCONTINUED

L9 is orange. Despite the project having been included in the Infrastructure Development Plan of 1997, the line remains unfinished. It has been constructed in two sections, north and south, and the gap between the two, the central section, is still pending, so that if one looks for the line on the Barcelona Metro map, the stations that have been completed pop out in their brilliant orange colour. But for the stations still in limbo, a less dazzling, faded orange is used, and the line linking them is broken and almost ghostly, consistent with the need to distinguish between what could exist and what actually does.

Can Zam, located in Santa Coloma de Gramenet, lies at the foot of a hill. As an escalator carries the walker up towards the colourful blocks of flats that stand out on the side of the Can Franquesa hill, he observes the scene and would like to say something, but then realises that he does not, in fact, have sufficient information to say anything meaningful. However, he makes an immediate correction: nobody really knows the meaning of the word meaningful. And then he thinks of the words of Vladimir Nabokov, 'Caress the detail, the divine detail', and that's what he focuses on, the details.

Every building is a new creation. There is no harmony, but this also creates a strange harmonious mix.

You can hear the radio blaring out from balconies – 'Good afternoon, it's two o'clock ... that's one o'clock in the Canaries' – followed by the news.

There is an unseasonal Father Christmas hanging from one of the balconies, even

LAURA FERRERO is an author, screenwriter and journalist whose articles and reviews have appeared in *El País*, *ABC Cultural*, *La Vanguardia* and *FronteraD*. She has published two collections of short stories with Alfaguara, *Piscinas Vacías* (2016) and *La Gente No Existe* (2021), and in 2017 Alfaguara released her first novel, *Qué Vas a Hacer con el Resto de Tu Vida*.

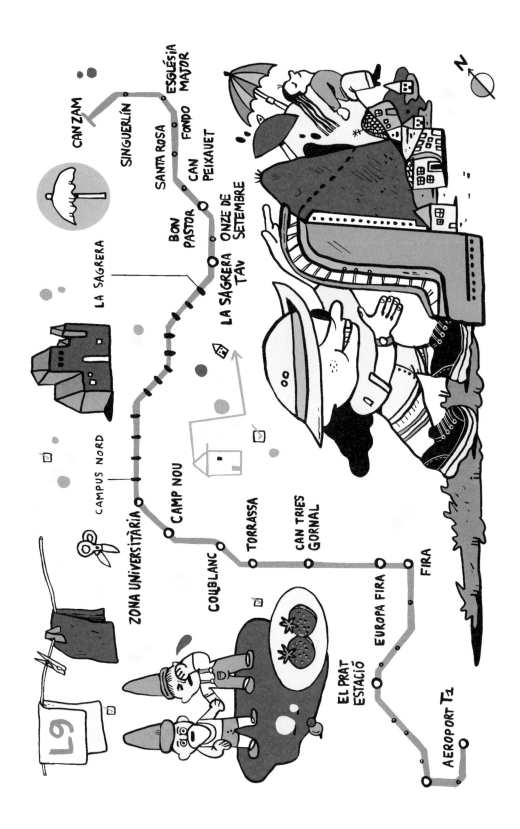

though it is 15 April, the red of his clothing faded by the sun, which reminds us that it is not winter.

At the entrances to these haphazard homes, decorative plaster figurines welcome the passer-by, and in one of the entrances two elves are holding hands on top of a column; one of them has a broken nose, and the walker invents or imagines the cause of such an accident.

As the saying goes, 'unless you invent things you're not alive', and, as he travels up the final section of the escalator, the walker allows himself to be transported by the aroma of clothes on washing lines, those universal banners of everyday life.

In the open space at the top of the escalator, there are several tables, each with a sunshade, accommodating pensioners playing cards and boardgames. Small children charge around (their grandchildren, the walker assumes) and sometimes they are allowed to throw the dice and move the counters on the board.

The L9 was created with the aim of connecting Barcelona with the metropolitan area via two branches: the Línea Sur was to go as far as the airport in Prat de Llobregat, passing through l'Hospitalet, and a second branch to the north would extend to Badalona, passing through Santa Coloma de Gramenet. Furthermore, this line would bring the metro to neighbourhoods such as Sarrià, which had never had a public transport service. Construction began on the L9 in 2003, the first section came into operation in 2009 and currently there are twenty-four stations in operation: nine on the eleven-kilometre L9 north section (La Sagrera, Onze de Septembre, Bon Pastor, Can Peixauet, Santa Rosa, Fondo, Església Major, Singuerlín, Can Zam) and fifteen on the south section (Zona Universitària, Collblanc, Torrasa, Can Tries/Gornal, Europa/Fira, Fira, Parc Logístic, Mercabarna, Les Moreres, El Prat Estació, Cèntric, Parc Nou, Mas Blau, Aeroport T2 and Aeroport T1).

THE PASSENGER   Laura Ferrero

THE FIRST EXPLORERS

Without any context, places are just places. The walker is surprised to read a poster announcing the proximity of an Iberian settlement. He reads it again, as if he had not understood. Located on top of a hill called Puig Castellar, the settlement is, for Santa Coloma, an emblem and a symbol of its identity. At an elevation of 303 metres, its excellent defensive position and commanding view over the surrounding territory lead the walker to believe that it must have been an important town from which its residents were in contact with nearby settlements. From those heights it controlled a long stretch of the coastline, including the Besòs estuary, the Barcelona plain and access to the hinterland towards Vallés.

In the distance, the city of Barcelona – an ants' nest that never stops moving – stretches out towards the sea. From the hilltop, with one foot in the remote past, the walker reflects on the first inhabitants to arrive there, to that city which was not yet a city, and compares those settlers with the early explorers. Explorers have always been lost, never having been to the places they were heading for. Nor did they expect to know precisely where they were, and, in fact, what allowed them to survive was a resolute attitude, perhaps a kind of optimism, when it came to believing they would find their way. It is that attitude, so they say, that enables civilisations and individuals to progress.

Sant Jordi, St George, is a truly international saint. In his Catalan guise he slayed the dragon in the town of Montblanc in the province of Tarragona, which is why Catalonia offers its thanks, celebrating la Diada de Sant Jordi (St George's Day) every 23 April, with festivities in every town in the region. There are countless traditions linked to the day, from the *sardana* (the Catalan national dance) to *castells* (the famous human pyramids). The day is also linked to roses (red, like the dragon's blood), lovers and, above all, to books: traditionally, a man would present his beloved with a rose and receive a book in return. Times have changed, however, and today it is more common for lovers to give each other roses *and* books, irrespective of gender, and the practice can extend to family and friends, much to the delight of publishers, as during the week of Sant Jordi more than 1.5 million books are sold (and many more roses). Not for nothing is Barcelona the publishing capital of Spain, home to a lively independent sector in both Catalan and Spanish and the headquarters of the leading Spanish publishing groups – although the largest, Grupo Planeta, has recently decamped to Madrid because of perceived uncertainty around the Catalan drive for independence. On La Rambla, the Passeig de Gràcia and other streets in Barcelona, as well as throughout the whole of Catalonia, the stalls set up for book signings attract long queues, while libraries and bookshops organise reading marathons of literary classics. The popularity of Catalonia's book day inspired UNESCO to make it a global celebration, taking advantage of the coincidence that the anniversaries of the deaths of both Shakespeare and Cervantes fall on 23 April – and, of course, the dragon's as well.

From the vantage point of that settlement, which has now become a tourist destination, the walker observes the aeroplanes crossing a cloudless blue sky as they head for El Prat Airport.

A BAR IN SINGUERLÍN

Apparently, the ◉**Singuerlín** neighbourhood was created thanks to a bout of bronchitis – specifically one that affected a wealthy businessman, Emili Singuerlín i Ros (1881–1942). During the 1920s this city councillor from a Catalan family of Alsatian origin built a summer house here, attracted by the healthy dry climate of this mountain area, which was exactly what he needed, and ended up lending his name to the district.

The neighbourhood was built entirely on the mountainside, and, despite the fact that some slopes are equipped with escalators, there are not enough of them to cater for all the elderly people who need to stop for the occasional breather on their way home. The walker greets them: a lady with a walking stick, opposite the church; an elderly couple who, dressed up in their Sunday best, are having a conversation in the Plaça Sagrada Familia.

In an alleyway two children chase after a cat, who eventually outmanoeuvres them by jumping over a fence and disappearing. And so the walker visits a succession of metro stations that, like the seasons of the year, define apparently imperceptible changes in the city: ◉**Església Major**, ◉**Fondo**, ◉**Santa Rosa**. He goes past a bar called Los Amigos and wonders how many bars there are in Barcelona with the same name – plenty, he imagines, and he stops at a different bar bearing the name Yosmar, where the waitress, Merche (so says the name tag on her T-shirt), serves him a beer. Blackboards hanging on the walls list the various tapas and types of sausage available, together with the house specialities, and, on a shelf that is impossible to reach, there are several adventure-story books with their covers facing out towards the clientele. The walker, who is short-sighted, asks Merche what the titles are. 'I don't know,' she says. 'They're not there to be read.' The walker mumbles in a voice loud enough to be heard, 'So why have books, then?' And we hear once more, from Merche's mouth, the best of all replies: 'Why not?'

The echo of those words pursues him on his trajectory, and the walker is astonished by the names of the shops and establishments: the One Love beauty parlour, which announces keratin treatments and improbable hair-straightening products; a halal butcher's; a friendly shopkeeper who, at number 9 Carrer del Rellotge, advertises his shop as selling 'modern Arabic clothing', opposite a fruit shop that still carries the sign of the previous occupants, 'Unifa Disseny'. Shops that have mutated into other shops, neighbourhoods living quietly, beyond touristy central Barcelona, lie in the path of our *flâneur*, who leaves in his wake the roundabout immediately outside ◉**Can Peixauet** station and is about to cross the bridge that links Santa Coloma with Barcelona. The aroma of orange blossom, the indisputable scent of spring, is pervasive.

CROSSING THE RIVER

In *Beauty and Sadness* (Vintage, 1996, USA / Penguin, 2011, UK), Yasunari Kawabata sums up the sense of loss as follows: 'There's nothing you can do. Waiting for Mr Oki is like waiting for the past – time and the river won't flow backward.'

The layout of the city is defined by rivers. If Barcelona finally wanted to look towards the sea ahead of the Olympic Games (despite the fact that it has never

The L9 platform at Can Zam.

stopped doing so), it has now set its sights on reclaiming its rivers. The history of the city's rapprochement with the two main rivers that flow into the Barcelona Metropolitan Area goes back a long way. The problem of the pollution and deterioration of the Besòs (a river that came to be seen as little more than an open sewer) and its immediate vicinity dates back to the 1960s, following the huge growth in the population in its surroundings and the process of industrialisation in those communities. The policy of repairing the damage to river areas began in the 1980s, promoted by the local councils and the Generalitat de Catalunya, and the river's condition was greatly improved; the cleansing measures

implemented in the 1990s to improve the quality of the water, which was heavily contaminated by industry and the urban population, were particularly effective.

Consequently, the residents of Can Peixauet can now watch their grand-children paddling in the river, something they would not have believed possible thirty years ago. In those days the Besòs stank as it made its way through Barcelona, and the few creatures that survived in its waters were almost suffocated by a visible toxic spume. Now, decades later, the Besòs River Park, a public space located along the final nine kilometres of the river's course, from its confluence with the Ripoll to the point at which it flows into the Mediterranean, is a reality, together with the sight of chil-dren tiptoeing across the river, flanked on either side by grassy banks.

For many, the Besòs represents the limit; for others, it means promise and opportunity. The city, like the river, like time itself, never looks back, and neither

The river Llobregat near the Mercabarna metro station and the airport.

THE PASSENGER   Laura Ferrero

A pensioner rests in the shade in the Singuerlín neighbourhood.

does the walker as he descends towards the Besòs River Park and, from there, looks up and marvels at the architecture of the bridges from below, an architecture that we never really notice because bridges are there to be crossed not for people to stop and examine them.

THE SAGRERA SCAR

As often happens in stories and in life, a wrong turn leads to the discovery of something unfamiliar not only about the world but about oneself. One of these occurs at Ⓜ **La Sagrera**, the last stop on the northern section of the L9. One of Barcelona's largest urban scars is, without question, the area occupied by the train lines between Sagrera and the city limits. Works started in 2009, but they were suspended between 2015 and 2018, and completion is not anticipated until 2023. Hundreds of metres of streets have been dug up and left half finished. Roundabouts, closed-off paths and fencing. The new station at Sagrera is a break, the most important infrastructure project in Barcelona since the Olympic Games, creating a fistful of possibilities, but whole neighbourhoods, lost in the break in the orange line, have been left in limbo.

So, setting out from Sagrera, the walker improvises or invents other routes, chances his luck along major roads and through back streets, a celebration of life and surprises. It's easy to get lost, to stray off the planned route and end up somewhere that you didn't know you really wanted to go.

As he arrives at Plaça de Sanllehy, the walker has a memory of something, but he's not sure exactly what. Was it around here that he spent his afternoons as a child? Is this where his grandmother would take him to the fountain, to the nursery called Espígol where he went with his grandmother the last time she voted, and his grandmother, a diminutive figure in the pressing crowd, said that the worst thing about growing old was becoming invisible? Wasn't it there, in the fruit shop on the Avinguda de la Mare de Déu de Montserrat, where his mother used to buy oranges because they were better than the ones from the Estrella Market? Wasn't it there that he fell over when he tried to jump over the metal railings around the steps? Wasn't it there that they started doing roadworks one day, and the whole park disappeared, swallowed up into the ground? And was it over there or over here where the children had to stop playing because they dug up the square to build the metro and no one could use it between 2007 and 2015?

The poet and writer José Lezama Lima said in an interview that 'a journey is an act of reacquaintance and recognising oneself', and it is possible that in both of these there is a form of spiritual brotherhood. A journey is a spatial movement, both real and symbolic, since we pass from one place to another but also from one emotional state to another and from one mode of thought to another.

So, suddenly the walker stops for a few moments to wonder if he has come all this way just to arrive at Plaça de Sanllehy, to remember a snippet of his childhood in a square that's no longer a square but rather the potential to be something else, a transport hub, via this metro line that will eventually connect up but for the time being is split, this L9 that will have fifty-two stops, twenty of them with links to other modes of transport, and a total of 47.8 kilometres of track, making it one of the longest metro lines in Europe.

And the walker continues his journey and discovers at the other stations nothing more than potentials, in the subjunctive tense, at some point in the future

'The L9 will have fifty-two stops, twenty of them with links to other modes of transport, and a total of 47.8 kilometres of track, making it one of the longest metro lines in Europe.'

(Ⓜ Sanllehy, Ⓜ Lesseps, Ⓜ Puxet, Ⓜ Mandri, Ⓜ Manuel Girona, Ⓜ Camp Nou), but just now he can't stop thinking of what motivates someone to set out from home and get lost. Maybe, despite the fact that rivers and time never travel backwards, the past is necessary to understand the ramifications of the present.

AFTER THE BREAK

Towards the south, after the central break, in which the stations can be guessed at from the construction sites and signs indicating a hypothetical completion date for each of the stops, the L9 begins again at Ⓜ Zona Universitària, on Avinguda Diagonal, the artery that forms the backbone of the city and divides it, as its name suggests, into two triangles.

But both sections of the line, north and south, merge in the walker's head; there is only continuity. As he passes the travelling fair at Ⓜ Collblanc he watches the children spinning on the roundabout because he has a feeling they might be the same ones that he saw in Singuerlín chasing the playful little cat who gave them the slip over a fence.

The walker leaves behind the hubbub of central Barcelona, L'Hospitalet, and now enters the exhibition zone where they're building those tall skyscrapers for people visiting Barcelona without going into the city itself, on whistle-stop tours and business trips to the suburbs of what could be just any other city.

He is now getting near to the other river, the Llobregat – which flows between two stations, Ⓜ Mercabarna and Ⓜ Les Moreres – another river that Barcelona has revivified, integrating it into the city and putting paid to its ill-fated status as a forgotten waterway.

The main problem with the Llobregat is its salinity, and, although it is true that levels have improved, it is still not yet possible talk about a full recovery. By the 1970s the run-down final stretch of the Llobregat was a sewer, devoid of life. It recovered part of its natural condition in 2008 thanks to an environmental restoration and landscaping plan, which aimed to open up the riverbank to the residents of the ten municipalities through which the Llobregat wends its way. The result is that today the local population no longer lives with its back turned on the river, and it has become an area much frequented by pedestrians, cyclists and joggers.

Arriving at Ⓜ El Prat station, the walker continues into the town of the same name, the ante-chamber to the airport, and, just as in Plaça de Sanllehy, he is gripped by a sense of déjà vu, and his grandmother comes back into his thoughts and tells him they have to go to El Prat to buy something. He doesn't remember what, but he doesn't have to strain his memory too hard because a statue in the Plaça Pau Casals reminds him: chicken, the *pollo de raza Prat*, bred exclusively in this district, the only

Spanish breed of chicken, characterised by its blue legs, to receive a Protected Designation of Origin from the European Union.

The distant aroma of his grandmother's chicken stew, or chicken with pisto, accompanies the walker as he arrives at the Sant Cosme district, and a few hundred metres further on he loses himself along a road adjacent to a small canal off the Llobregat along which he leaves behind civilisation and concrete.

Now he is surrounded by the green and brown shades of cultivated fields. The streets are replaced by smaller roads, and opposite him as he crosses the B.203 he spots a green embankment that he mistakes for an ordinary park. But as he approaches it he realises that it is something else, that people do not just come to this park to go jogging or for a kickabout. He pauses to observe this army of people who, armed with binoculars, are staring up at the sky.

Then the penny drops. Up there, pot-bellied planes appear over the horizon on their final approach to ◆Ⓜ **Aeroport del Prat**. Equipped with apps such as Flightradar, people point to indistinguishable dots, which get bigger as they approach. 'Vueling, Amsterdam–Barcelona' or 'Emirates, Dubai–Barcelona', says one. The plane-spotters put their hands over their eyes to make improvised sunshades and carefully watch the trajectories of these black dots, which, with a roar that becomes increasingly audible, make their approach until their wheels touch down. Welcome. And the children, in their parents' arms, wave to the passengers they can imagine behind those windows but cannot quite see.

Barcelona is a city visited by almost twelve million tourists each year (this statistic is from 2019, the year preceding

The pollo de raza Prat, the El Prat or Catalan chicken, is one of the few breeds of poultry to have survived without cross-breeding, having been selected by the earliest breeders in the El Prat de Llobregat area of Barcelona Province. Over time its reputation has grown and grown, making it an icon of the region and a gastronomic celebrity. The annual December fair, the Fira Avícola de la Raça Prat, not only turned this strange chicken, with its white 'ears' and blue feet, into a show breed but made it a symbol for the people of El Prat, who are proud to share a nickname with the bird: *pota blava* ('blue leg' in Catalan). Raised in the open air and fed on cereals and natural products without using any hormones, the meat is tender and particularly flavoursome, with a high protein content and little fat, so any meat eater thinking of visiting El Prat de Llobregat, a destination largely absent from most popular tourist itineraries, already knows which local speciality to try. In spite of the high quality of *pota blava* chickens, however, the farming sector has changed a lot over the past fifty years, so to ensure farmers continue to rear this native breed – but, above all, to support current production levels – a new generation needs to take over, and this is not happening. In response, the local authority has provided funding for new farms and to explain and pass on the whole process with the aim and hope of attracting new recruits to the business and making a traditionally seasonal product, such as the El Prat chicken, available all year round, a bit like out-of-season fruit and vegetables – but in the chiller cabinet.

A boy watches
aeroplanes land from
the 'viewing point'
near El Prat Airport.

the pandemic). These tourists occasionally walk around the city armed with guides and blogs that claim to reveal the secrets of 'Barcelona in Two Days' or 'Barcelona if You Have Only 24 Hours', forever reducing the city to a standardised formula, an obligatory itinerary with no surprises, in which the city becomes a must-see checklist so you can say that you've been there, seen that, the Mecca of the contemporary tourist.

It is here, at the El Prat plane-spotting area, that the walker decides to stop. He makes a decision not to go any further because there are things one should do at least once in a lifetime – for example, look at things from the other side, stay and admire the planes landing at El Prat.

The walker screws up his eyes, looking momentarily at one of the plane-spotters, and, once again, he thinks it might be one of the pensioners who was sitting on a bench near the Plaça Sagrada Familia. Could that be possible?

But, as we've said, there's no need to go into all the details, so our walker looks back up at the sky, and, as he does so, he tells himself that our motivation for doing things remains hidden and opaque. Perhaps he had only arrived there to welcome the new arrivals enthusiastically, to immerse himself in the pleasure of welcoming and to embark on the return journey with a sense of promise, a sense that everything is always just beginning. ✈

SUPERBLOCK 503

The regular, octagonal blocks that make
up the grid of streets in the Eixample
district turned out to be perfect for cars,
transforming Barcelona into a noisy,
polluted city. But they also lend themselves
to a new experiment in low-cost urbanism,
the superblock, which aims to 'pacify'
the city's spaces and return them to the
people – as well as to plants and animals.

GABI MARTÍNEZ
Translated by Kathryn Phillips-Miles

A superblock in the Eixample district,
at the crossroads of Carrer del Parlament
and Carrer del Comte Borrell.

It all began with sound. After more than forty years living in Barcelona I thought I had reflected a lot on my city, on how its design and character influenced my life, but it was only when I started to lose my hearing that I could really explore our relationship – and it made me wonder whether we actually had a future together.

I had gone to the doctor with some hearing problems, and the tests showed that I was becoming deaf in one ear, so a few weeks later I had a platinum stirrup bone implanted. I left hospital with my ear bandaged with a cushion of gauze and dressings that were supposed to muffle the impact of sound for a few days. I had only walked thirty steps along the street when an ambulance sped past me, four metres away, with its siren at full volume. I felt a crack in my temple, and I nearly fainted. I had gone deaf in the ear that had just been operated on.

I recovered my hearing a few weeks later, but that awful experience triggered a whole series of questions and answers that caused me to look at the urban ecosystem in a different light.

According to some statistics I live in the noisiest city in the Western world and the seventh noisiest in the world in a ranking topped by Guangzhou, New Delhi and Cairo. The data are relative, because it's anyone's guess who the interested parties behind the statistics might be, but no one can dispute the existence of uncontrolled environmental noise. In Barcelona, 44 per cent of people's homes are exposed to high noise levels, particularly those caused by vehicles, each one of which emits seventy decibels, even though the city's by-laws limit noise levels in the street to sixty-five. In addition, it is predicted that with the ever-increasing use of headphones with the volume turned up as high as it will go and the general tendency to normalise excessive noise, one in ten young people will suffer incapacitating hearing loss by the year 2050. Studies suggest that these days an inhabitant of Barcelona has the hearing of someone sixteen years older than their actual age.

Despite that, these studies also state that the environmental factor people are least concerned about is noise. Moving traffic is the main emitter of decibels within cities, but because people treat it as simply background noise, more complaints are generally triggered by ventilation systems or night-time hospitality venues. The car has enjoyed total impunity thus far because it is viewed as being an essential tool, so vital for millions of citizens that they would rather go deaf at an early age than seriously consider life without a car or even just using it a little less often. Therefore people living in Barcelona have decided to ignore the noise made by the 600,000 cars that drive into the city centre from the suburbs every day (more than in Manhattan) to make up the six million daily journeys that are undertaken there.

These are the things I've been thinking about since the day I went deaf. I also wondered why ambulance sirens are

GABI MARTÍNEZ is a Spanish journalist and writer known both for his fiction and non-fiction. The English-language edition of *In the Land of Giants: Hunting Monsters in the Hindu Kush* (Scribe, 2017) was a runner-up for the Society of Authors' Premio Valle-Inclán Award, and his novel *Las Defensas* (Seix Barral, 2017) was selected as best book of the year by several Spanish newspapers and media. In 2021 Destino published his book on superblocks, *Naturalmente Urbano*. His work has been translated into ten languages.

so loud and why that particular one was switched on right outside a hospital where ear operations are carried out. How do you design a city? Who are the people considering this? Really considering it?

In my search for answers, Salvador Rueda came to the fore. He is a biologist-psychologist who, as someone who does hear traffic noise, has come up with an urban design not only to decrease environmental noise volumes but also to reduce other polluting emissions by taking away space from heavy vehicles and increasing green spaces. His design is called the *supermanzana*, or superblock, and it's transforming the city.

Salvador Rueda, who came up with the idea of the superblock, at home.

*

When you fly over Barcelona as you come in to land, the way the heart of the city is ordered is striking. It is divided up into long streets and avenues that cross the city between clusters of buildings with identical perimeters. Each one of these is a block. The plan adopted to roll out the new Barcelona was the brainchild of Ildefons Cerdà. Each block measures 113.3 metres on each side, the corners being cut away in a chamfer to create an octagonal footprint. The interior of the block is a large neighbourhood space used for parks and gardens, terraces, public and private patios. The blocks are genuine islands that are impermeable to the outside world, and that's why they are called *illes* (islands) in Catalan.

Cerdà rose to prominence with his design; he was a visionary who was able to provide space for moving traffic in wide, airy streets while at the same time giving the inhabitants quiet spaces where they could mingle. Although he foresaw a future with motorised transport, the sheer number of vehicles that would soon overwhelm the city eluded him. All these solutions were no longer applicable during the 1960s when uncontrolled development began to destroy Barcelona's skyline. Then the end of the dictatorship and financial optimism stimulated by the prosperous car and motorcycle factories turned the car into an object of desire, a symbol of success.

So in 1987, when Rueda came up with the idea of reinventing Barcelona based on a model inspired by the mathematical-naturalist legacy of Cerdà (which, among other things, consisted of reducing the number of cars moving around the city), it was not a success. The car industry provides thousands of jobs. Smoke means progress and modernity. And what on earth *is* a superblock?

'What a name, it sounds like a joke,' says a resident of the Poblenou neighbourhood who has taken part in several demonstrations against superblocks, 'because now I have to park my car two streets away from home.'

Let's return to the plane flying over the constellation of the Eixample district, the large area built in the late 19th century around the old city, which was the first to be developed according to Cerdà's plans. To sketch out a superblock we need to

The first attempt at a superblock was in 1993, in El Born, a neighbourhood of narrow streets between the Barri Gòtic and Barceloneta that never suffered from heavy traffic. In the absence of a specific urban plan, the initiative involved pedestrianising the area, which led to rapid gentrification and an invasion of tourists – better than the previous neglect, though, if not necessarily a successful urban development. Superblocks two and three, on the other hand, were more deliberate and far-reaching interventions. Both in Gràcia, they involved the pedestrianisation of certain streets, a reduction of the speed limit in others, the removal of one-way streets and bringing the road level up to that of the pavement, all initiatives designed to change drivers' habits and provide equal access to the streets for all means of transport. Gràcia lent itself well to experiments in urbanism; for centuries, up until 1897, it was an independent municipality with distinct characteristics in terms of culture and the built environment. The smallest of Barcelona's districts, it is also one of the most densely populated, and by the early 2000s was already crowded with tourists, who were confined to the narrow pavements. According to a study conducted before and after the implementation of the superblocks, pedestrian movements increased by 10 per cent and cycling by 30 per cent, while car traffic fell by 26 per cent. Most importantly, residents embraced the change, and despite a huge increase in tourism – with consequent gentrification – no one has seriously considered reintroducing traffic to the streets of Gràcia.

group together the original blocks in a square of three blocks by three, the nine blocks making up a larger block – a super-block. Some 6,000 people and 480 legal entities (from shops to associations, institutions, law firms, cultural centres and so on) reside within those 16,000 square metres. Then the secret lies in the regulations: to reduce both the moving traffic and its speed to ten kilometres per hour within the area. The superblock supports children playing in the street, urban gardens, leisurely strolls.

'They are pacified areas,' says Rueda as he walks among a group of children kicking a ball about in the middle of an avenue in Poblenou. There are planters dotted around on the asphalt, which has been painted and marked out for games.

Many thinkers on local town planning use this warlike term to refer to car-free areas in a city that in 2021 registered 667 annual deaths from pollution of various types – 163 of these attributed to noise, as it happens. It seems like a strange reason, too ethereal, but Rueda knows that noise is the cause of the most unrecognised disease of the 21st century, and that the discomfort it produces, that feeling of not being quite right that is so difficult to quantify, has an impact in terms of neurovegetative alterations as well as hormonal and structural changes. People

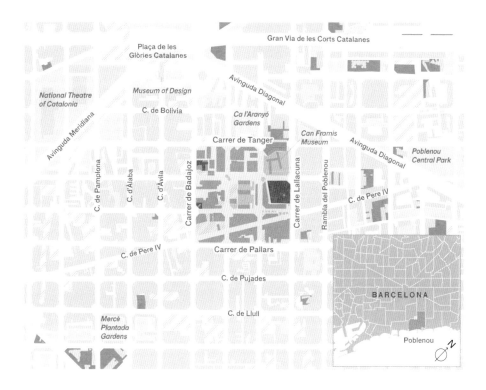

Gran Via de les Corts Catalanes

Plaça de les Glòries Catalanes

Avinguda Diagonal

National Theatre of Catalonia

Museum of Design

C. de Bolivia

Ca l'Aranyó Gardens

Carrer de Tanger

Can Framis Museum

Avinguda Meridiana

Avinguda Diagonal

Poblenou Central Park

C. de Pamplona

C. d'Àlaba

C. d'Àvila

Carrer de Badajoz

Carrer de Lallacuna

Rambla del Poblenou

C. de Pere IV

C. de Pere IV

Carrer de Pallars

C. de Pujades

BARCELONA

C. de Llull

Mercè Plantada Gardens

Poblenou

who are subjected to excessive noise suffer from higher blood pressure, greater incidence of cardiovascular disease, over-stimulation of neurotransmitters. All this is reflected in the proliferation of diagnoses such as insomnia or stress. In 2021 Spain took more tranquillisers than any other country in the world.

*

There is a genuine conflict taking place. The car lobbies are squaring up to those who hope to reconquer the walkable city in the so-called 'battle for space' – a dispute that was triggered in 2016 when the city council in Barcelona decided to experiment with a superblock in the Poblenou neighbourhood. Before that, superblocks had been introduced in Gràcia and El Born, older areas with narrow, labyrinthine streets where the traffic is negligible. I live in Gràcia, right on the edge of the superblock, and there is often an almost rural calm, although the rest of the area is also quiet. However, Poblenou has straight, wide streets for free-flowing

Just another noisy day in Barcelona.

'Five years on, green spaces have doubled in area, and 176 trees have been planted. The 2,218 cars that passed through on a daily basis have dropped to 932.'

traffic. Experimenting with a superblock here represented a kind of pilot scheme before bringing in superblocks in the rest of the city. That would mean turning back the clock and reducing vehicular traffic by around 15 per cent.

Right from the word go, the Poblenou pilot scheme met with harsh criticism from the media, a significant part of whose income depended on the advertising revenues from different car brands. Several newspapers devoted their front pages to complaints from residents. Radio and television covered protests and offered reasons why the city should withdraw from the scheme immediately. Surveys were cited that showed that 87 per cent of residents were against superblocks. The city council was harshly criticised for supporting such madness, and many of my friends agreed that superblocks were a populist idea that would not resolve anything of any import. Some of them, who lived outside the city, asked why they should give up their cars when they reached the city limits. They alleged that, in the first place, there were simply not enough car parks to accommodate all the cars coming from elsewhere on a daily basis, and, what's more, what would they do if they had to transport something heavy within the city? No, no way. During the first few weeks the city planners dealt with the complaints and problems that arose and made adjustments for inaccuracies and ambiguities while spreading the word about how people could make new use of the street. Some residents suggested including a children's playground, a picnic area, table tennis tables or a *pétanque* terrain. These requests gradually began to find their way into the media.

'Superblocks gaining supporters in Poblenou,' was a headline in one newspaper in 2017.

'Successful car-free scheme that began with neighbourhood opposition,' another reported in 2018.

'700 fewer deaths a year: the impact of superblocks' – 2019.

'Superblocks, or how to return the city stolen by cars to pedestrians' – 2020.

Five years on, green spaces have doubled in area, and 176 trees have been planted. The 2,218 cars that passed through on a daily basis have dropped to 932. The shopkeepers' hostility to the 'experiment' that would apparently have destroyed their footfall has dissipated, and they're optimistic about the new shops opening up in the area, an increase of 30 per cent. Now that the banners against the superblock have been taken down from balconies, Rueda's words have a powerful and singular ring about them: 'If you want to know what the effect of superblocks is, first of all you have to ask the people who are against them. Next, the people who are in favour. Last of all, you have to ask the people who have been living in them for ten years.' Two years would have been quite long enough for the residents of Poblenou.

When it comes down to it, a pacified area is one where pedestrians have taken over from cars and where you can hear

The streets highlighted in these maps are those open to traffic. The first map shows the current status, the second the plan developed by the municipality of Barcelona (known as 'Green Streets') and the third the much more radical model that the inventor of the superblocks, Salvador Rueda, would like to see applied. With thanks to Salvador Rueda for the maps.

Current Situation

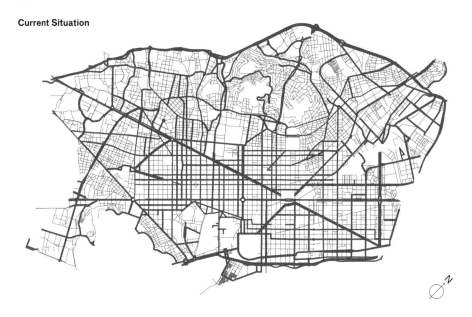

The 'Green Streets' Project

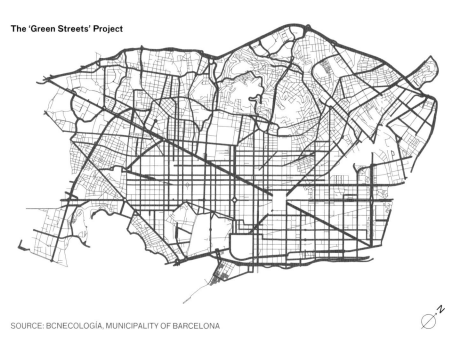

SOURCE: BCNECOLOGÍA, MUNICIPALITY OF BARCELONA

Superblock 503 Model

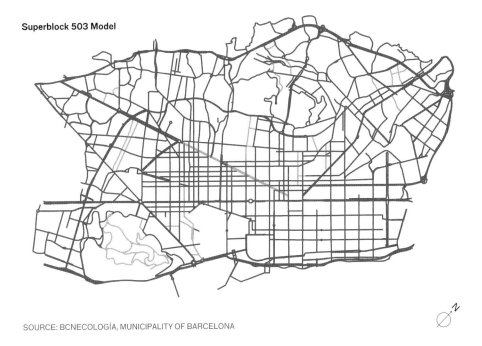

SOURCE: BCNECOLOGÍA, MUNICIPALITY OF BARCELONA

birds singing in the street. But the fight goes on. A few months ago I interviewed Lluís Puerto, head of the Royal Automobile Club of Catalonia (RACC). The RACC is an association created to give assistance to drivers, and it is also the diplomatic wing of the car industry. 'Does your association lobby to exert political pressure?' I asked. 'The last thing the RACC would do is to get involved in politics,' he said. 'And what about as a group exerting social influence?' 'The RACC doesn't want to lay down the law for society. We aim to adapt to society and to introduce elements of objective good judgement. If society is tending to become less tolerant of pollution and towards the need to reclaim our public spaces from cars, we wouldn't argue with that because we all agree that we want clean air, zero accidents, trouble-free journeys, no breakdowns ... these are objectives we can all share. How you get there and the speed at which you get there, that's where there's more confrontation. The key is the speed at which you get there.'

A few days later I got a call from the RACC's press office asking me not to include this interview in my book, as some of the questions made them uncomfortable. There are many architects, town planners, ecologists, journalists and so on who point out the obstacles put in their way or even overt censorship when they publish or try to disseminate information in favour of restricting car use in the city. Pressure from the press office did not stop me from including the interview, however, but it is clear that the RACC intends to take urban transformation in a (very) calm manner. In the meantime, Rueda lays emphasis on the urgency of the environmental crisis: pollution alerts are becoming run of the mill, and that's why the city changed its slogan from *Barcelona,*

More green means less asphalt, which, in turn, means less dust and toxic particulate matter released by the friction of millions of tyres on road surfaces. In Barcelona, this particulate matter accounts for almost half the atmospheric pollution. The toxicity is so acute that, as well as combating it by planting more vegetation, traditional asphalt is being replaced with permeable surfaces that allow rainwater to filter through. These areas smell fresher and cleaner, and those of us who go out for an early-morning run really notice the difference. When it comes to renaturing, rooftop spaces are the icing on the cake. The costs involved in creating green rooftops are high because many buildings need to beef up their structures to support the weight of vegetation and water, but Barcelona is covering any empty space, however small, from narrow ditches to broad flower beds, with grass, trees and many other plants, creating a network of healthy microclimates. A good covering of green on a rooftop guarantees warmer buildings in winter and cooler buildings in summer. Rooftop spaces can also be transformed into green allotments in the sky. Barcelona had fifteen allotments that were cared for by retired people chosen through a lottery system, but environmental warnings have attracted horticulturalists of all ages, and vegetables are now being grown in the most unlikely corners of the city. There is a deluge of applications for permission to set up community allotments, and if no more permits are being granted it is down to legal constraints. This legislation is due for an urgent update to facilitate the proliferation of places such as Terrat d'en Xifré, a cluster of green rooftop spaces that includes fish ponds, insect hotels, urban kitchen gardens and ten thousand native plants from forty different species spread over six connected buildings. The result is a wild garden where you can breathe clean air while contemplating the nearby sea. (G.M.)

Make Yourself Beautiful! to *This Is Not a Rehearsal.* Superblocks can be introduced quickly, cheaply and effectively and offer instant rewards. To begin with, it is sufficient to amend street signage, change the directional flow of some streets and introduce more planting.

What is more, Cerdà's futuristic design means that the city can easily be adapted to modern times. The historian Joan Tort is so fascinated by the fact that the design is still relevant that he has drawn up a walking itinerary to show his students how to think about a harmonious city, the value of proportions, real sustainability. Tort begins the tour on foot beside the modernist Sant Pau Hospital, located right in the middle of Eixample, and walks down towards the sea. It takes five hours, and he stops on the way at places such as the Casa Elizalde, where the interior island is often used by reading clubs, art workshops, conferences.

At the Torre de les Aigües, Tort says, 'Listen.'

The silence takes you by surprise. An oasis in the heart of the metropolis.

'The balance between public and private space is striking,' says my guide.

A few streets further down, the University of Barcelona takes up two blocks. Walking through the lush vegetation in the large internal courtyards, Tort points out 'an extraordinarily pioneering fact that is hardly noticed today: the implicit idea of a garden city. Not many people know that in this double island, the proportion between built space and green space is almost 50 per cent.' That ideal proportion intended for the blocks in Eixample is now a feature of the superblocks.

Proportion and balance are the key elements for transformation to be successful. How many superblocks are needed to change the character of the city? Today there are six in operation. One reference point is the Mercat de Sant Antoni superblock. It is located on the border between the modernist Eixample and the old city. There is not one car. There are terraces everywhere, people sitting on benches, children chasing each other down what was once a road and is now a pedestrian pathway made of porous asphalt to reduce the island-heat effect that in the summer can increase the temperature in the city by as much as 8 degrees Celsius.

The trouble is that most of the superblocks are too far away from each other, and for there to be real change they need to be joined up. While they are still few and far between, the undeniable improvement in the quality of life that a superblock brings with it means that property companies are rushing to increase the prices of the flats and houses within it, pushing out those residents who are unable to meet the higher rents. That's why the people against the scheme believe that it is a solution for the rich. 'Some residents don't want superblocks, not because they don't like them but because they don't want to be next out after all the cars,' says Laia Grau at the council's town-planning department. Grau rejects the theory that cleaning up the metropolitan area means separating thousands of people from the places they have lived in for decades. She believes that emotion matters and that people from every stratum of society should be able to live in cities and that accessibility should be a fundamental right for those on lower incomes, too.

That's why work has already started to bring as many superblocks as possible into operation simultaneously. Politicians are hoping that this will make life difficult for speculators and believe that they would not dare to increase prices city wide, or

The Barcelona model of the superblock has been studied by urbanists all around the world to see if it could be applied elsewhere. The superblock design brings with it a different understanding of the urban environment: streets are transformed from places of transit into public squares where people can walk and use the space. But excluding traffic from large parts of a city risks simply moving the congestion elsewhere, so studies on the applicability of superblocks look at those factors that would result in less disruption to city mobility. The conclusions are that superblocks need to be planned in densely populated areas, in which a large proportion of the people can make use of the spaces that are freed up and in which there is access to public transport and/or private modes of transport, such as bicycles. It also helps to have a city laid out with a regular street plan, as Barcelona is. Admiration for the Catalan city's project has led to feasibility studies and the first concrete initiatives, primarily in Europe. There are no definitive projects yet, but the idea has aroused the curiosity of numerous architects, and Vienna has begun a pilot scheme and plans are under consideration in Stuttgart and London, where a vast area could be pedestrianised right in the centre, encompassing universities, theatres and museums. The superblock solution would also seem right for New York, particularly in certain areas of Manhattan where residents often don't own cars and yet the streets are always clogged with traffic.

at least not as much as they might have done with a long-drawn-out scheme and disconnected superblocks. In the event that this is achieved 'there won't be any more talk about superblocks', says Grau, 'but rather it will all be about *a* superblock, one single superblock, because that's what the whole city will be'.

Rueda says that if the council sets its mind to it, Barcelona could have 503 superblocks in operation in four years' time. The entire city transformed into one single superblock 503. 'With €200 million, which is not a great strain on municipal funds, you could turn everything around. It's not an illusion: it is calculated down to the last euro.'

The problem is that there are still too many influential and powerful players who want to stop this from happening, and those politicians who wish to bring about transformative change are coming up against insurmountable obstacles. The architect David Bravo has had several articles critical of transportation blocked. Over breakfast in a café, Bravo says that in order to reveal the hidden reality behind the worthy word 'sustainability' you simply have to consider the following contrast: on the one hand, when a car-free day was introduced across the city for twenty-four hours it was the target of a torrent of criticism and almost no one abided by it; on the other, ten days are devoted to the Automobile Barcelona car show, which is almost unanimously welcomed because it boosts the local economy.

*

The *Eixos Verds* (Green Corridors) scheme is one way of shaking off some of the commercial pressure without stopping the transformational plans. These are long streets and avenues where there is a new dedicated lane (until recently used by cars)

Quiet time in the Eixample superblock.

'We residents are used to using our streets for leisure purposes. We frequently occupy the main streets in the city on Saturdays and Sundays to buy and sell soap, honey, cheese, fruit and vegetables.'

for bicycles, scooters, light vehicles and even pedestrians. Trees have been planted along these corridors, there are urban gardens, support has been given to shops selling local products and to activities at ground level. The *Eixos Verds* are not a substitute for superblocks, but they lay the physical foundations for when the latter are finally introduced or when wholesale transformation can be brought in.

In any case, we residents are used to using our streets for leisure purposes. We frequently occupy the main streets in the city on Saturdays and Sundays to buy and sell soap, honey, cheese, fruit and vegetables. On Saturdays and Sundays dozens of portable market stalls are set up on streets all over my neighbourhood, including Carrer Gran de Gràcia, the main road. This also happens at the Creu Coberta–Sants intersection. One street that crosses the city, the Carrer d'Aragó, has already been opened up to the public (and closed to cars) several times. A band called Aurosmith, whose members are some of the parents from a local school (named Auró), has performed right in the middle of this six-lane highway. They play pop songs and they also plant 'urban' runner beans. One of the band members, Dani Nogués, has not only been involved in looking after the allotment in the Carrer del Consell de Cent, but he's also taken aubergine, courgette and pepper seeds up to his eighth floor flat where the allotment continues. Miriam García, the

head of Landlab Laboratorio de Paisajes, has placed her trust in residents such as Nogués to green the city. García believes that hundreds of residents are becoming green champions and that they have the knowledge and desire to green the island where they live and, as a consequence, green their superblock and their city. The facts show that she is right. Encouraged by the proliferation of these enthusiastic volunteers, García seeks green solutions that will oxygenate this high-density city, and she sees the superblocks as an opportunity to replicate gardens such as the one at the intersection of Enric Granados and Consell de Cent in Eixample.

Increasing green spaces is a priority both to absorb carbon dioxide (three times above the permitted level) and reduce the average temperature in the city as well as to create a decent network of sound absorbers, because the trees, plants and bushes act as natural baffles. However, any old green is not enough. Supporting native plants is yet another change in direction in the environmental policies of a city that up until four years ago chose flowers and plants based simply on how beautiful they looked. Someone who is so close to this subject that they did not wish to be named told me, 'Until very recently the Parks and Gardens Department was not governed by ecological criteria. Those spaces were designed by managers.' In view of the clear lack of balance, the department has started listening to ecologists and biologists differently, and 160 hectares of green space (with as high a proportion of native plants possible) are being added to the almost 1,200 hectares that already exist in the city. At the same time weeds are being defended as a source of biological diversity. 'It's all a question of mentality. There are no bad weeds,' says Coloma Rull, who, although she has been working in environmental jobs for many years, is still surprised by the number of letters and emails that Barcelona residents send to her department and to the media complaining about appearances that they believe are down to neglect. Hostility to apparently uncontrolled green spaces together with the pleasant certainty provided by a lawn being regularly cut sums up the attitude in so many cities where people like something that has methodical and clear borders but not something that looks a little wild; where something good is associated with care and something bad (I'm exaggerating a little) with people who have more freedom than they deserve. As nature doesn't fit this pattern, now would be a good time to discover that perhaps we should all be a little more wild. What are the consequences of walking on the wild side? Glyphosate, the herbicide that has caused so many problems for decades, is being used a lot less. The city of Barcelona is replacing invasive plants such as *Pennisetum* and mock orange with better-adapted native species such as *Viburnum tinus* and *Cistus albidus*. Pansies and cyclamen grown in greenhouses are being replaced with local grasses that last longer, attract more pollinators and fauna and, unlike non-native plants, do not need to be replanted at the end of the season.

'Some people burst out laughing when we talk about insect hotels,' says Rull, who is in favour of increasing these refuges visited by lacewings, earwigs, bees, wasps and other key pollinators for strengthening the native plants that are being grown in the city once more. There is also a plan to save ten species of orchid that have been battered by wild boar, those new hooligans moving into the outskirts of the city.

The proliferation of vegetation must allow some animal species that abandoned the inhospitable city to return. In 2006 Barcelona drew up a plan to introduce corridors that would, for example, allow a squirrel to cross the urban landscape from the Ciutadella Park very close to the sea to the Serra de Collserola Natural Park. The scheme also attempted to stop the gradual isolation of the natural environment in a city that was turning in on itself and focusing on its attractiveness to tourists and whose growth was also isolating the Collserola mountain range as it was becoming increasingly strangled by the pressure of property development within Barcelona itself and on the other areas on the periphery. The division between countryside and city became increasingly stark: the city was the city, the countryside was the countryside and never the twain shall meet. What were the results of the 2006 plan? Nothing, as it was never put into action. A bird flying high in the sky over Barcelona can see a lush natural island besieged on all sides by concrete and asphalt. The height of anti-ecology. Squirrel numbers are rapidly decreasing. The same is true of badgers. Wild boar often root around in the rubbish bins in the mountain neighbourhoods, adapting to human pressure. Birds are doing the same, and the philosopher Marta Tafalla, who regularly takes walks around Collserola, says in her book *Ecoanimal* (Plaza y Valdés, 2019) that birds 'have a serious problem: our cities are

very noisy. The noise we generate makes it difficult for birds to hear each other. We are flooding nature with noise pollution that is annoying, bothersome and chaotic. We are not filling dumb nature with our profound language; we are not providing voiceless nature with the only voice that is allowed to express itself, but rather the complete opposite. We are turning off nature's voices and replacing them with noise.'

*

The hope now is that superblocks will create favourable conditions for finally opening up corridors in Collserola, including reducing the decibels. Noise reduction is at an advanced stage, and superblocks are in the vanguard. The first step was to improve the bus network in an attempt to reduce traffic. The improvement had an effect on other networks, and now the city benefits from an agile and efficient public transport system. The municipal bike-hire scheme, Bicing, has made bicycle usage shoot up, and there are now 272 kilometres of cycle lanes. Every member of my family under fifty travels around by bike, whether traditional or electric. My seventeen-year-old son swapped his bike for a scooter a few months ago. A friend of his who had just bought a new one gave it to him. Today the cycle lanes are full of scooters, and you have to move around even more carefully because, after what the journalist Miquel Molina has called 'a tsunami of scooters', the city is a hotchpotch of mini-vehicles

'Superblocks are the ideal foundation for making the fifteen-minute city (one in which you can get almost anywhere in that time) a pollution-free reality.'

(there are also motorised or non-motorised skateboards, classic scooters and monocycles) that squeeze around corners unexpectedly. Although some urbanites still have much to learn about semi-slow travel, new traffic regulations were brought in this year, and superblocks are the ideal foundation for making the fifteen-minute city (one in which you can get almost anywhere in that time) a pollution-free reality. Molina himself rides a bicycle, and it takes him exactly fifteen minutes from his home to the office. 'But I'm lucky enough to live in the city centre, where I work,' says Molina, aware of the difficulties faced by workers who live in the suburbs.

Making Barcelona accessible will be key to the introduction of superblocks. If there is quick and relatively comfortable access, the scheme may persuade many of those who are reticent, and this will facilitate the execution of the scheme on a large scale. This is what has happened in Vitoria-Gasteiz, a city in the Basque Country. It is much smaller than Barcelona, but it is determined to transform its appearance, following the 'fantasy' dreamed up by Salvador Rueda. The residents of Vitoria-Gasteiz quickly saw the benefits of the first noise-free, green streets and were almost all in favour. Work has already started to pacify the entire city.

In November 2021 the UN used the example of superblocks as a way to combat climate change. The UN stressed that superblocks can be used to regulate street temperatures, how immediately the effects are felt, and that people can feel an affinity with their natural environment. 'The point is to start using all our senses again. In the city we seem to use only two of them: sight and hearing,' says Tafalla on a walk around Collserola.

The philosopher is anosmic, meaning she was born without a sense of smell, and perhaps that's why she focuses so much on the other senses. Her binoculars are hanging around her neck, as today she wants to study birds. 'I find jays fascinating. They're really boisterous. They perch in different trees, but they never stop talking. What on earth are they saying? I love watching them and thinking about them. Looking out for them sharpens my other senses.'

According to experts, we have at least fourteen senses, not just the classic five, and contact with nature awakens our animal core and lets us activate them all. Children instinctively seek out nature because they want to understand themselves as biological beings. What is more, superblocks place them, place us, place nature on the threshold of providing car-free, safe routes that will allow some children to go to school on their own, supervised by shopkeepers, hospitality workers and support staff. Barcelona's residents have spent many years becoming specialised as urban beings, but the city now seems ready to remind us that we can still be human beings and feel like human beings ... *within* the city. 🐦

El Raval: The Capital of a Country that Doesn't Exist

Catalans have always associated El Raval with freedom, a place to escape from bourgeois life into a colourful souk, but, as this exploration of Barcelona's quintessentially multi-ethnic neighbourhood shows us, those who live there often do so out of necessity rather than choice.

NAJAT EL HACHMI
Translated by Kathryn Phillips-Miles

A greengrocer in Carrer de Joaquín Costa, El Raval.

**DIFFERENT WAYS TO GET
TO THE NEIGHBOURHOOD**

Since my family and I moved to the Gràcia neighbourhood, one of our favourite outings is to stroll down Carrer Gran to the Jardins de Salvador Espriu. From there, we either carry on down the Passeig de Gràcia, with its wide pavements, or we turn right to enjoy the elegance of the Rambla de Catalunya. I grew up in a much smaller town called Vic, about sixty kilometres from Barcelona, but the capital city of Catalonia has always exerted an influence on me that is difficult to describe. I guess it must be the same thing that draws millions of tourists there every year, but for those of us who spent our childhood and adolescence in poor neighbourhoods inhabited mainly by immigrants, the big city is like a chimera, a place bursting with promises of freedom and anonymity, something that is an inaccessible luxury for people banished to the outskirts – or to the outskirts of the outskirts – where everyone knows everyone else. I am aware that this anonymity is one of the things that many people hate most about big cities. 'The thing is that in Barcelona people don't even know their next-door neighbour's name,' is something my friends from inland Catalonia often say to persuade me that I made a mistake in moving here. But for those of us who have ever experienced the asphyxiating control of a community where no one is a stranger, where you feel like you're permanently on show (especially if you happen to be a woman), that's exactly what we want. In this case, anonymity almost amounts to class aspiration. Even more so if we bear in mind the fact that people don't usually emigrate from one country to another, they move to where they know someone, and that's why whole villages or whole neighbourhoods in the country of origin end up moving to villages or neighbourhoods in a host country. When my mother talks to me about the people from the Rif (the area of Morocco from which we came) who live in Vic, she reels off a whole list of relationships of how who is related to whom (rooted in our village of origin, Beni Sidel, Nador), one that she knows off by heart, as if she had every family's genealogical tree in her head, while I barely know how many cousins I've got and which one is whose child. (In my defence, there are rather a lot of them; I think I have more than fifty cousins by blood.)

So, strolling along like *flâneurs*,

NAJAT EL HACHMI was born in Morocco in 1979 and moved to Spain in 1987. Her bestselling first novel, *L'Ultim Patriarca* (2008), won the Ramon Llull Prize and the Prix Ulysse and has been translated into eleven languages, including English (*The Last Patriarch*, Serpent's Tail, 2010). It was followed by the novels *La Caçadora de Cossos* (2011; *The Body Hunter*, Serpent's Tail, 2013), *La Filla Estrangera* (2015) and *Mare de Llet i de Mel* (2018), all of them bestsellers internationally. In 2019 she published the feminist essay *Sempre Han Parlat per Nosaltres*, and her latest work is the novel *Dilluns ens Estimaran* (2021), winner of the Nadal Prize for the Novel.

'A country made up of different elements of many other countries brought here by its inhabitants, resulting in a landscape that is full of contrast both on the urban and human levels.'

wandering by instinct, flowing downhill like a stream, is one of our greatest pleasures. We rarely go beyond Plaça de Catalunya, because after that it's the realm of mass tourism, and the real inhabitants are being pushed out. Even so, I do sometimes keep going and occasionally venture off to the right to one of the neighbourhoods that may not be a literary part of town but has the most literary references in the whole city, where the occasional legendary corner is associated with famous writers who mention it in their works. This is El Raval, with its narrow streets, its chaotic, hectic atmosphere, where the pedestrian is hit by an improbable number of different smells as if they were in some exotic country, a country made up of different elements of many other countries brought here by its inhabitants, resulting in a landscape that is full of contrast both on the urban and human levels. When they talk about this area, people often mention pre-1992 and post-Olympics Barcelona, because that great sporting event brought about sweeping changes in the city and its structure. I once found the concept of 'Barcelonisation' being used as a synonym for gentrification. I have no memories of my city prior to its great transformation apart from in descriptions of it by writers. I recommend *The Gray Notebook* (New York Review of Books, 2014) by Josep Pla if you want to get an idea of Barcelona at the beginning of the twentieth century, as viewed by a young student who is learning to become a writer by keeping a journal, written during the months he

was unable to attend university because of the 1918 flu epidemic. I can't imagine what El Raval would be like without some of the great cultural centres that were built after 1992, the Barcelona Museum of Contemporary Art (MACBA) or the Centre of Contemporary Culture (CCCB), for example. I do remember when there was a wide-open space where the Faculty of History and Philosophy now stands because I used to go to a tea shop right opposite (there's a cake shop there now that offers vegan, gluten-free cakes). Some believe that these buildings really improve the state and appearance of a neighbourhood that's always been rather grotty, but groups that are against mass tourism are highly critical of this attitude and say that, in fact, the changes have made no difference to the people who actually live in the area.

It's not so hard for me to admit that the critics are right, because just a quick glance at this part of El Raval allows you to see a series of micro-worlds existing side by side that don't seem connected – in fact, just the opposite. The two thousand people attending US philosopher Judith Butler's lecture in the Plaça de Joan Coromines during the first Biennial of Thought don't appear to have any contact whatsoever with the flip-flop-wearing tourists buying paper cones of sliced ham in the Boqueria Market; the people heading out to an independent cinema to watch cult films aren't likely to cross Carrer d'En Robador where prostitutes tout for business. I don't think that people going to

Posing for the camera (**from left to right**): a couple in the Rambla del Raval;
a man in Carrer de Valldonzella; a prostitute near Carrer d'En Robador;
a young man on his lunch break on the Rambla del Raval.

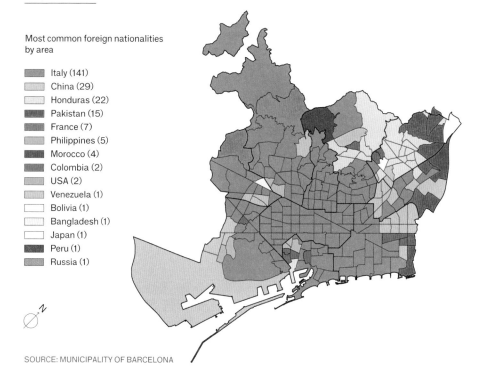

Most common foreign nationalities
by area

- Italy (141)
- China (29)
- Honduras (22)
- Pakistan (15)
- France (7)
- Philippines (5)
- Morocco (4)
- Colombia (2)
- USA (2)
- Venezuela (1)
- Bolivia (1)
- Bangladesh (1)
- Japan (1)
- Peru (1)
- Russia (1)

SOURCE: MUNICIPALITY OF BARCELONA

Italians in Barcelona are the city's largest immigrant community, and their numbers keep on growing. This phenomenon has been seen right across Spain for decades; the country has attracted large numbers of young Italians (not always well educated, so it does not constitute a brain drain) looking for work and an environment perceived as welcoming and similar in terms of climate and lifestyle but with more job opportunities – so much so that even during the toughest periods of the economic crisis of the 2010s, the Italian community in Spain continued to expand, a distinction only shared by the Chinese community. Nowadays Italians constitute the largest group of foreigners in Barcelona's wealthiest neighbourhoods and form part of the city's economic fabric in all kinds of ways: one of the most popular occupations is the operation of cannabis clubs, in which members can legally consume marijuana, but many also work in the restaurant sector or start-ups, often founded by expatriates themselves. Someone has also opened an Italian bookshop in Barcelona, Le Nuvole,

The foreign population of Barcelona (2021)

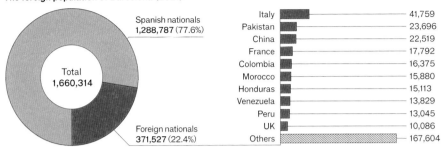

Spanish nationals
1,288,787 (77.6%)

Total
1,660,314

Foreign nationals
371,527 (22.4%)

Italy	41,759
Pakistan	23,696
China	22,519
France	17,792
Colombia	16,375
Morocco	15,880
Honduras	15,113
Venezuela	13,829
Peru	13,045
UK	10,086
Others	167,604

The foreign population of El Raval (2021)

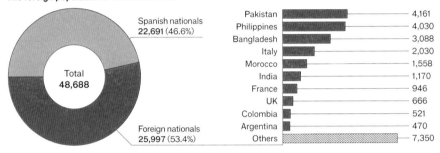

Spanish nationals
22,691 (46.6%)

Total
48,688

Foreign nationals
25,997 (53.4%)

Pakistan	4,161
Philippines	4,030
Bangladesh	3,088
Italy	2,030
Morocco	1,558
India	1,170
France	946
UK	666
Colombia	521
Argentina	470
Others	7,350

SOURCE: MUNICIPALITY OF BARCELONA

which sells to the large Italian community but also to Catalans interested in the language. There are numerous success stories, which are the focus of much celebration. An exhibition held in a public park in the city centre in 2021 showcased more than thirty successful Italian women, such as the star architect Benedetta Tagliabue, who designed the Spanish Pavilion for Expo 2010 in Shanghai, and Caterina Biscari, director of the Alba particle accelerator, the city's imposing – and extremely costly – research centre.

Friday prayers in the crowded mosques are even aware of the existence of the Sikh temple in Carrer de l'Hospital. I often go to El Raval for talks at the CCCB, to buy books in La Central bookshop but scarcely establish any contact with the Pakistani residents or the skateboarders zooming around MACBA's wide-open space or the groups of teenagers who use CCCB's piazza to rehearse their incredible dance routines; for those of us going to the talks, these are all part of the natural landscape.

'I felt that everyone was staring at me, and I was on the point of confronting a man who was looking at me really hard when he decided to talk to me. "You're the writer, aren't you?"'

The fragmentation of today's societies, something we tend to attribute to social media, is, in fact, the way in which many neighbourhoods are structured in the West. A glance at the polyglot, polytechnical and fragmented El Raval shows us that this mosaic (like Gaudí's *trencadís*) is an intrinsic feature of cities in a globalised world, and that most citizens spend their time crossing invisible borders (or not). The UK-based academic Nira Yuval-Davis employs the accurate term 'everyday bordering' to refer to this as it relates to immigrants.

A FRAGMENTED NEIGHBOURHOOD, SPLIT IN TWO

An invisible border that divides the El Raval neighbourhood in two is the *rambla*, or boulevard, that bears its name. From the crowded Ramblas to the Rambla del Raval, we encounter tourists from across the globe. I sometimes like to stop and simply listen to the passers-by. It is one of my secret pleasures to see which languages I can identify, which dialects, try to make guesses at the languages I haven't got a clue about and lose myself in that flood of sounds that demonstrates that Babel was never a curse. It is the languages that are really diverse in this torrent of people from all over the world, but if we look at what they're wearing, what really strikes you is how similar their clothes are.

I must confess that for me the Ramblas (to which I sometimes head to go to the opera) will never be the same as it once was. This emblematic Barcelona street was forever scarred one fateful August afternoon in 2017, in the same way that the World Trade Center was scarred one 11 September, Atocha Station in 2004 and the *Charlie Hebdo* offices in 2015. Just recently I walked through the Boqueria Market and ended up at the space behind it. The images of a young man captured by the security cameras immediately came into my head. He was someone whose appearance, name and way of moving were extremely familiar to me, as he was, like me, the child of Moroccan immigrants. But Younes Abouyaaqoub and the others involved in the attacks on Barcelona and Cambrils in 2017 are nothing at all like the boys in my neighbourhood, because in my neighbourhood no one would ever have dreamed of mowing down pedestrians on the Ramblas in the name of God or Islam. Yet Younes not only dreamed of it he actually carried out his macabre plan on 17 August 2017 at 4.56 p.m. A few minutes later my family and I left home to walk down to the centre, taking our usual route. We stopped when we started getting messages warning us to be careful as there was a terrorist on the loose. We decided to stay within our neighbourhood, meet up with a friend to comfort each other, and while we were waiting for her at a café I started feeling strangely guilty. Why? Because the terrorist was a Muslim, and my parents and brothers are Muslim, too? I felt that everyone was staring at me, and I was on the point of confronting a man who was looking at me really hard when he decided to talk to me. 'You're the writer, aren't you?' We had a good laugh about it with my friend, and I will always remember that moment of laughter.

WHERE ARE THE WOMEN?
I mentioned earlier that El Raval is divided in two, and on the right-hand side (as you look towards the sea) there is a lot of activity that has nothing to do with tourism. There are many people out on the street because the flats are small and overcrowded. There are also people who live on the street itself. Some homeless people have erected their makeshift shelters on the Faculty of History's piazza. There are halal butchers and Lycamobile top-up shops where internet cafés and food shops used to be. There are men out on the street, lots of them standing around in groups, talking loudly. It is almost always men out there on the street, replicating in Barcelona the dynamic of the separation of spaces typical of our countries of origin. There are generally few Pakistani women to be seen, although there are many people from that country here. The women who are out on the street are the mothers going to or coming back from school with their children or the girls who help out as teaching assistants. Many teachers tell me that they tend to disappear suddenly to get married in their country of origin. Unfortunately, arranged or forced marriages are still the usual practice, and not only among Pakistanis. Even more girls have gone abroad, as this is one of the few ways to emigrate: many

Gràcia is home to Barcelona's largest Roma community. The first to settle in the neighbourhood – more specifically at Carrer de Francisco Giner 49 – were the Valentí, a family of Roma wool traders who arrived from Florence in the early 19th century with their cattle and horses. They were not the first Roma family in Barcelona – there were other communities in neighbourhoods such as Sant Andreu and Horta – but they were the first of many to move to Gràcia, in the area between Plaça de la Vila and Plaça del Raspall. The Roma were very important in shaping Catalan cultural identity from a number of perspectives. They were, for example, responsible in the 1960s for the creation of Catalan rumba, a genre of street music influenced by rock and Cuban music, the greatest exponent of which was Peret, who represented Spain at Eurovision in 1974. As the Roma integrated they suffered repression twice over: on the one hand, as elsewhere, they were persecuted for their ethnicity; on the other, they had to deal with the policies of the central government, which prohibited or limited the use of Catalan, their language of choice along with Romani. The two languages ultimately combined to create Caló Català, a hybrid language in which the vocabulary and phonetics of Romani sit alongside Catalan grammar. Unfortunately, however, Caló Català is now in decline, like the other Roma dialects of the Iberian Peninsula. Younger generations use it less and less, and their mother tongue is, to all intents and purposes, Catalan.

families 'give' their daughters in marriage to close relatives so they can get a visa and come over here. As I write these words I am still upset about a recent crime. Two women of Pakistani origin who lived in Terrassa (a town within the metropolitan area of Barcelona) were brutally murdered by their brother in Pakistan because they wanted to divorce their cousins, whom they had been forced to marry. This is the most extreme expression of a kind of violence against women that is still normalised behaviour for many Muslim men. There is progress, and I am convinced that a change in attitudes will come, but it's costing too many lives.

As I watch these groups of men, I imagine that there is an inaccessible El Raval where the women are shut up in their homes as if they lived in a harem, although without the seductive and enchanting orientalism portrayed by Delacroix or Catalan artists such as Marià Fortuny and Josep Tapiró.

A few years ago I made a radio programme that was commissioned by the state radio network for their cultural station. It was a news bulletin in Amazigh, my parents' language and one of the most widely spoken languages in Catalonia, perhaps ranking number three in numbers who speak it as a mother tongue. It was a real challenge. I had never even heard a programme in Amazigh, a language that is only used orally, and, of course, I had never seen it written down or used it myself in my writing. It was an interesting experience. In my search for people to interview, I came across a short stretch in Carrer de l'Hospital where there were three businesses run by the same family from the Rif. There was a restaurant, a butcher's and a barber's, and they were all called Mediterráneo. I went into a bar to have a cup of tea and realised this was an out-and-out transgression. To this day it is completely unacceptable for a women to go into a café or a bar in many villages in Morocco as well as in many neighbourhoods with a majority of immigrants from my country of origin. That is why in that clean and spacious café, where the tea was steaming as it was being poured and the food smelled like my mother's, there were only men. I was aware of the looks and the silence as I went in, but I was served in a friendly way by the owner, who was very happy to be interviewed. It became a little oasis for me, somewhere I could go when I was missing harira soup or a tagine or delicious remsemmen. One day I asked the owner about the cooks, and he told me that they were all women from his family. I asked if I could go and say hello to them, and I met a large, quiet group, busily cooking in a scene reminiscent of the patio of the adobe house in which I grew up. A group of women cooking together, with their faces reddened by the heat, their roomy dresses with the sleeves rolled up and the hems of the skirts fastened around their waists in a knot. They spoke to me in low voices, and I remembered all the advice we were given when we were little – not to catch the attention of the men by talking loudly or shouting. When I walk through the streets of El Raval, I imagine that other invisible city, the city of women and their gatherings in their homes, the industrious lives of diligent wives, and I wonder who will write their stories.

NO ONE EMIGRATES TO EL RAVAL
A few years ago in Rabat, I was lucky enough to meet Juan Goytisolo, the writer from Barcelona, thanks to a mutual friend who arranged a dinner so that we could get together. I admit that I was fascinated by that somewhat shy man with his calm voice and intense gaze. He was interested

in my life's journey. Although we were from completely different generations, we had both taken the same route but in the opposite direction: he set up home in Marrakesh after having lived in many other places, fleeing the suffocating post-war atmosphere and his bourgeois family, and I moved to Barcelona, fleeing from an immigrant neighbourhood and a working-class family. The types of neighbourhoods in which Goytisolo felt at home were hostile environments from my perspective. By then I had published a couple of books in Catalan, Goytisolo's native language, but one that he never used for his writing. I don't know if it was because of his age, but I had the impression that the elegant musicality of his speech (even though it was a friendly and informal conversation) and the hint of something melancholic in his prose were reminiscent of the sounds of the terrible times that my generation have only heard about. Or perhaps simply that well-known feeling of not being from anywhere and not being able to fit in anywhere was reflected in his way of looking at the world. I wondered, what is a Spaniard doing living in Morocco when so many of us have fled the country? But Goytisolo felt at home in Marrakesh, where he lived for the last few years of his life and set up his own family. Thanks to him, Jemaa el-Fna Square has been awarded Intangible Cultural Heritage status by UNESCO.

I must confess that the first I'd heard about Goytisolo was not through reading his articles in *El País* or his well-known novels; in fact, I saw him on television when I was about nine or ten years old. I can't quite remember how long it had been since my mother and my brothers and sisters had moved in with my father in the cold, foggy town of Vic; two or three years perhaps. Two or three years of

silence vis-à-vis our native country; back then, immigration from other continents was rare, and our immersion into Catalan society was total. No smells, no music, not one element in our environment connected us with the village we had left behind. This was all a long time ago, the end of the 1980s or the early 1990s, but I can clearly remember the emotion I felt when I heard the melody emanating from our old television set in our damp living room, an emotion aroused by discovering a kind of nostalgia of which we weren't even aware. After the introductory music, Goytisolo started talking about that part of the world that was never talked about even though it is separated from Spain by a strait barely fifteen kilometres wide. To be more accurate, there was the occasional piece of news about Morocco on state television, when Juan Carlos I and Hassan II had meetings. It was surprising that the king of Spain, the head of state of a parliamentary democracy, would appear on television and say that Hassan was his brother, but back then these things weren't discussed, there were no comments. Complete silence. Silence bequeathed by terror in the case of Morocco and its authoritarian king; silence bequeathed by the consensus established during the transition away from dictatorship in the case of Spain.

The programme was called *Alquibla*, and it reported extensively on the Muslim-Arab world. It was directed, presented and narrated by Juan Goytisolo. It should be remembered that the world progresses at different speeds as far as communication is concerned. Although there were places at the beginning of the 1990s where the internet was already being installed or where second-generation mobile phones were being sold, neither electricity nor running water had yet reached Beni

Left to right: A typical souvenir shop near La Rambla; a barber plies his trade; a little shop in Carrer de l'Hospital; an employee at the Museum of Contemporary Art cleans the building's walls.

Sidel, Nador, and the telephone would take another couple of decades. Our lack of connection with anything to do with Morocco was not complete: we sometimes went to Barcelona on a train that operated as it had done for a hundred years, and after undertaking some administrative formalities at the consulate (which was then in the Rambla de Catalunya) or at the government delegation, we used to wander around the narrow streets of a Barcelona that didn't seem like Barcelona – at least, not as far as our vague idea of this mythical city (mythical for those of us who came from a village where so many families had a man living there, although not 'exactly' within its limits) was concerned.

The bustling neighbourhood into which we followed our resolute father was crowded with people, was sometimes hard on the nose and seemed more like an Arab souk. Many years later I would learn to name it and locate it both on a physical map and on a worldview map generated by literature. El Raval – previously also known as the Barri Xinès, or Chinatown – often appears in the world described by a wide range of writers, both in Catalan and Spanish, and it always represents a point of escape – anarchic freedom – since it is an area that is free from the orderly streets found in the bourgeois Eixample district. Goytisolo himself wrote a book devoted to the wanderings of the writer Jean Genet in this quarter, where he survived thanks to help from neighbours and by prostituting himself. For people coming here from the bourgeois, upper parts of the city, the poverty and unbridled life might have seemed attractive. In fact, this is still happening, even in the 21st century: some young people from rich families spend a gap year not travelling through exotic and dangerous countries

but by joining anti-establishment squatter movements that are fighting shoulder to shoulder against the many evictions that are carried out on a daily basis along these streets; the extraordinary battle to halt the deterioration of certain buildings caused by drug traffickers is part of the argument put forward by some social movements. In this sense, managing to squat a drug trafficker's flat is almost a military conquest. The difference between the young people from the bourgeois areas and the poor immigrants, however united they may be in the struggle, is that the former can go home to their clean, comfortable and spacious homes while the latter have nowhere to which they can return.

A BUTCHER'S SHOP AS AN EMBASSY

For the immigrants in the rest of Catalonia, El Raval was a place where we could stock up on products that held a special place in our sensory and emotional memory, a memory that risked disappearing if our lack of connection with Morocco were to continue. Back then there was the odd halal butcher's and a whole host of products such as spices, tea or – once we had video recorders – VHS tapes with recordings of Moroccan musicians and comedians. Some years later it was possible to eat in halal restaurants in Barcelona, although they were run by Pakistanis, and the food had nothing in common with our cuisine.

The fact is that in the popular imagination of people both from Barcelona and Catalonia, El Raval is an immigrant neighbourhood, something along the lines of a capital city for all those who have recently arrived. This view is in stark contrast to that held by those of us who have actually experienced this process: no one who wants to move to an advanced, modern, western-European city does

Everywhere has its own derogatory terms for people from elsewhere, especially in places where there have been significant waves of immigration: in the USA, for example, there are names with varying degrees of disparagement implied for almost everyone (Limeys for Brits being one), and in post-war northern Italy, the land of the *polentoni* (polenta eaters) became home to millions of *terroni* ('peasants' from the south). In Catalonia, *xarnego* is a term for immigrants who arrived from southern Spain during the economic boom years. The word entered Catalan in the 16th century via the Gascon language to refer to the children of one Catalan and one French parent, but from the 1950s onwards it started to be used to refer to internal migrants. Now that their children and grandchildren can speak Catalan, the word *xarnego* refers more generally to all those who, despite living in Catalonia, tend to speak only Spanish, which is common, for example, among the members of the large Latin American communities that have grown up since the 1990s, particularly on the outskirts of Barcelona. One high-profile *xarnego*, often 'forgiven' in spite of his linguistic 'backwardness', is footballer Lionel Messi. (In contrast, the Spanish speaker Andrés Iniesta is happy to give interviews in Catalan, something he does with aplomb.) Still on the subject of derogatory terms ... Internal immigration in the 1950s and 1960s resulted in a demographic boom in the Barcelona region that created serious traffic issues in rural areas at the weekends. Country roads became clogged with the cars of visitors from the big city, and the daytrippers were often forced to answer the call of nature at the roadside; the resulting term *pixapí* ('pine pisser') is still used by Catalans in rural areas to describe city dwellers, particularly those from Barcelona. (S.B.)

so thinking they will settle in the area between the Ramblas and Avinguda del Paral·lel – El Raval. No one coming from another country freely choses to live in an area such as this, even though everyone thinks we prefer narrow streets to wide boulevards. Almost all the foreigners who live here do so because they are unable to afford a home in other parts of the city. As soon as they can, they leave. That's the reason, more than any other, why El Raval is a transient district. Back in the days when what I wanted more than anything in the world was to be able to live in the expensive city in which I was studying, I would never have chosen those winding, bustling streets. I was fascinated rather more by the open spaces of Eixample with its grand buildings with high ceilings.

I think I disappointed Goytisolo a little at that dinner in Rabat. He asked me where I lived in Barcelona and was surprised when I said Eixample. 'Don't you like El Raval?' he asked. The thing is, what represents freedom to some people can feel like a prison to others.

Enrique
Vila-Matas

The Mapping
of Paradise

We all have a street we have walked down a thousand times, where everything has a name. For Enrique Vila-Matas it is the Paseo de San Juan. In two pieces written thirty years apart, he revisits the landscape of his childhood, drawing a literary memory map and refamiliarising himself with his city following the forced isolation of the pandemic.

Translated by Simon Deefholts

91

LA CALLE RIMBAUD
1995

Someone who knew Kafka recalled that 'Once, when we were looking out of the window at the Old Town Square, he pointed out several different buildings and told me, "That was my school, and over there, in that building that stands out from the others, was my university, and a little over to the left, my office." Within this tiny circle (and he traced a couple of small circles with his finger) my entire life is enclosed.'

Yesterday I returned to the Paseo de San Juan, retracing the route that I have followed more often than any other in my life – some fifteen thousand times, I estimate, and I'm not exaggerating. It's engraved on my memory, but it only survives in my memory, in my recollection, because nowadays this legendary, formative route from home to school (along Calle del Rossellón and Calle de Valencia, connected by the Paseo de San Juan) is nothing like it used to be, reaffirming the words of Baudelaire that to outlive the city of your youth is a modern experience.

The world, the map of the planet – which I call *my Calle Rimbaud* – began on the mezzanine floor of number 343 Calle del Rossellón and ended at the corner of Valencia and the Paseo de San Juan, the location of the Marist school, previously a Salesian convent, which may have been the source of our inherited terror: a flock (to borrow a line from Félix de Azúa) moulded by the school desk and the prisoners' dock.

It was an intense walk, armed with satchel and a chocolate drink (always served cold) on a winter's morning: a short, magical and absolutely wonderful journey but as brief as childhood itself. It only survives in my memory, and for me it still represents the whole world, the map of the planet. Because everything else, everything that was off track, was a blank space with barely any significance, rather like the desert space that always attracted Rimbaud, for whom, not unimportantly, the land that eroticised his wonderful poetry needed a well-defined path, a street that it is said he had imagined since his childhood, a world glimpsed from a tender age that extended from a stretch of railings up to the patchwork colours of the harbour, which had to be (and for Rimbaud this was absolutely essential) out at the edge of the desert, which was what truly attracted him.

In the *Calle Rimbaud* – as it was called by the chubby poet José Lezama Lima writing in Old Havana – offered up as a 'secret wild pomegranate', the poet's whole world was encapsulated: the cathedral, the rebellious teacher's house, the school, the Turkish hats, the bookshop, cockades, liquor as strong as molten metal and, at the end of the route ('it has to be the edge of the world if we take another step'), the squirrel in a wicker cage that he saw as they set sail on a Danish frigate.

We all have our own *Calle Rimbaud*, and everything there has a name. If we stray from it, everything becomes unfamiliar, and we know that we'll reach the edge of the world if we take a step forward to discover it, if we try to go beyond the path from home to school, beyond our own unique recognisable world. We all have our own *Calle Rimbaud*, and if there is one thing that unites us all (speaking from my current perspective, from my position on the edge of the desert) it is a certain wonder that we experienced in childhood when we walked along it, because of the street itself and because at that age we are living in a natural state, uncontaminated, in a state of innocence. At that age we all possess a touch of wonderment, but the path of childhood, like the path from home to school, is short and wintry, and only too soon truth makes its appearance, what we call reality, which doesn't take long to force us to try to feed, as best we can, on the remains of that original wonder we once enjoyed, which has been taking its leave of us impassively, cruelly and sarcastically, slowly and for ever.

In my case, the map of paradise, my *Calle Rimbaud*, was once a secret wild pomegranate that stretched along six vital points on my Paseo de San Juan, six spaces that I can still visit in my memory in the same way that as a child I would navigate slowly with my finger on the maps in my atlas (the borders always marked in yellow): the submarine light of the entrance to my parents' home, the dark and gloomy bookshop run by the old Jewish man, the dazzling Cine Chile, the abandoned bowling alley, the mysterious home for the deaf and dumb and, at the end of the route, the railings around the school church.

The entrance to my parents' home looked forbidding when seen close up, but not so much so when I viewed it from a distance when returning from school, because then it acquired a certain strange coloration that was, nevertheless, typical of the world of Jules Verne and the entrances to buildings in Barcelona's Eixample district, with their decorative iron doors and steamed-up windows that, from a certain distance, gave me an exciting sense of underwater murkiness.

At number 341 Calle del Rossellón, in the bookshop belonging to the old Jewish man, something 'muffled in the distance' lingered on, the still-recent tragedy of a people pervaded the shop, and you could also inhale a strong smell of varnish, incense and the aroma of far-off countries, of rare commodities that I imagined were hidden in the inaccessible room at the back: sparklers, magic coffers, music boxes from Nuremburg (the city from which the old Jewish man had fled), rare books, sad folders full of engravings and strange stories.

Opposite the old man's shop there was a blaze of light from the lobby of the Cine Chile, announcing grand events, forthcoming screenings, Hollywood epics and, at night, Cinemascope. And beyond the cinema, but not as far as Calle de Provenza, was the abandoned bowling alley from which, on hot summer evenings, we could hear (or we children thought we could hear) the echoes of old Republican dances. And even further along there was a mysterious building that seemed to have come out of a fairy tale, a bit like a medieval castle, which was actually a modernist construction containing yet another enigma: the residents. We had been told that they were deaf-mutes, but we never actually saw anyone who lived there.

And finally, leaving behind the mystery of the silent castle, crossing Avenida Diagonal, there was a stretch of railings that, having seen them so often, had become quite familiar to me, until one day I saw them in a different context, and I was suddenly struck by the legacy of the Civil War, a legacy of horror: some photographs from the summer of 1936 in which, skewered on those railings, you could see a row of mummified nuns' bodies that had been housed in the building since before it became a school.

This legacy of horror would mark the beginning of the end of my childhood and state of wonder. With my first step into the desert and the discovery of reality, everything started to change, and ever since it has never stopped changing and, what is more, never stopped getting worse. Advancing into the desert of life has proved to me that, in the end, almost nothing of our world remains standing, nothing of the backdrop that was unique to us, nothing of our treasured *Calle Rimbaud*, where our whole world existed and which now, simply, *is no longer there*.

No, almost nothing remains. Yesterday I returned to the Paseo de San Juan, retracing the route that I have followed more often than any other in my life and which helped me to construct my own literary world to such a great extent. It's engraved on my memory, but it only survives in my memory, in my recollection, because this legendary, formative route from home to school has changed. It has been changed deliberately and not exactly for the better. Where there was an entrance full of submarine light, there is now only a new concierge who naturally does not know me and who asks why I'm staring so intently at him and the doorway. As for what used to be my home, today (to use another metaphor from my childhood) it is more like the Bleak House that Dickens wrote about. The mysterious castle is still there, now being used by a Catalan bank as their cultural centre. And the railings in front of the school church are still there, their tips just as sharp (as if they were lances) today as in time of war.

But not the least vestige remains of the other key elements of my literary map, my *Calle Rimbaud*. The Cine Chile is now an ordinary car park. The old man's bookshop is now the disgusting Poppy's Snack Bar. And as for the abandoned bowling alley, the old Republican echoes have given way to a tasteless, funereal homage to money: a dull, grey, provincial bank in crisis.

It is a strange panorama left after that lost battle in life, by which I mean childhood. Someone once said that growing old has its charm, that it is the same as learning to dance in one's youth, submitting to a rhythm that is a metaphor more non-existent than our inexperience. Perhaps. Growing old also has its advantages – to quote William Carlos Williams: 'the descent beckons as the ascent beckoned'. And, by way of example, the ability to enjoy Cervantes to the full can be offset against the lost ability to play with toy soldiers. Furthermore, we no longer have to go to school, and we don't wake up in the middle of the night frightened by the sound of the wind. Growing old may have its charms, but it is also true that growing old serves to show that we have walked the earth and that time has walked alongside us. It serves to show that we have advanced across shifting sands that have not led us further than the end of a pleasant path and that have placed us at the edge of a desert where, looking back and trying to recover something from our *Calle Rimbaud*, we can only see an old path in which Time, now at the very threshold of the desert, has written the abrupt end of our world, of the world itself.

BARCELONA, FLOWING DOWN
TO THE SEA
2022

I wander through what I like to think is the same neighbourhood where, one evening, on the Feast of Sant Joan, Pijoaparte, as he was known, jumped out of the shadows and walked along the Carretera del Carmel until he reached the Plaza Sanllehy. It is here that I arrived just a moment ago and from where I propose to go down to number 546 Calle Sardenya, which used to be home to Captain Blay – a victim of the Civil War and clear-sighted in his madness. Afterwards I'll cut across the AstroTurf pitch of Club Deportivo Europa, with which my father was once associated as a friend of the enterprising Zalacaín (briefly president of the club) to the extent that I became a member when I turned fourteen years of age and sometimes came third in my class and sometimes second (I could never quite break out of that particular loop). One Sunday morning, an extraordinary one for me, I saw Europa play, and all I can remember is my father, Zalacaín (with a gigantic Havana cigar) and a centre forward called Rojas. Did I want to be a centre forward? I doubt it, because at the age of five, in a game between the boys from Sant Andreu de Llavaneres and the then fledgling 'colony' of holidaymakers from Barcelona, I was sent off in the first minute for turning on their battle-hardened centre back following a tackle.

Before long I've also put the Travesía del Mal behind me, as I stroll down the Torrent de las Flors (which is really called Calle del Señor Torrente Flores), a key artery of Juan Marsé's imaginary neighbourhood, a neighbourhood that was always a subtle mix of the suburbs of La Salut and El Carmel, El Guinardó and Gràcia. I carry on walking, and at the same time I notice the proximity of Eixample, Barcelona's darkest area, the very place where Carmen Laforet set the lugubrious atmosphere of *Nada*, her implacable millimetric portrait of the Catalan bourgeoisie, and where Roberto Bolaño, a writer of genius, occasionally wandered as the ghost of Hamlet's father.

My feet start to drag, and I stumble (admittedly only in my imagination) down Torrente, knowing that once I have cleared the Plaza Rovira my line of sight will be even more crowded with the grandchildren of the defeated, of those 'men of iron, forged in so many battles, now weeping in the corners of bars'. I stumble, now almost in a straight line, towards the territory of my childhood, the Paseo de San Juan; I estimate that I'll get there at sunrise, just as the day is dawning.

The Paseo de San Juan, which I once called *my Calle Rimbaud*, always sends me back to the grey landscape of post-war Barcelona, with a solitary figure centre stage, a thin, wretched, bored schoolboy: me, in other words. A lonely figure whom I associate with a remark by Ricardo Piglia on the anguish and emptiness of the early years of his diaries: 'because there I struggle with a complete vacuum: nothing happens, actually nothing ever happens'. In my schoolboy diaries, nothingness also took centre stage. What else could I say if nothing ever happened to me? At this rate, I thought, I'll never get to be a writer. The horror of my empty days. I would never wish to return to that emptiness because, without the companionship of literature, I was reduced to a shadow.

'I am nothing but a shadow,' said Pepe Bergamín, one of my favourite writers at the time. The reason I tried so hard to escape that nothingness was because I didn't want to end up like an old (very old) Rimbaud who, in one of Le Clézio's novels, *La Quarantaine*, went into a tavern with the unmistakable appearance of a man without roots and was the very image of solitude as he made his way without the friendly company of literature.

I wouldn't return to those empty days even in a moment of madness, even if I were promised that, coming home from school in the evening, I would be able to see the submarine coloration of the doorways in Eixample once more. There, I thought, something must be happening – but I was never able to discover what that really was.

I have wandered further down, and I am now close to the Arco de Triunfo, where I'll take a detour to the very southern end of the Ramblas, which at one time meant everything to me and to everyone else. Those were times in which the only spectacle to behold was an extremely local population, a great river of humanity that flowed down to the sea, as one can still see in the great city of Naples.

In the past two years I've only been down to the south of the city on one further occasion. Two months ago I went to Drassanes in a taxi, and I was not exactly terrified, but I felt rather timorous, looking through the window in astonishment at the desolate – or should I say devastated? – urban landscape, an area that I was discovering with increasing bewilderment. It was all very strange, as if I had never seen it before. Suddenly, hearing the sound of wet tyres in the background, I looked out of the window, and I saw that it was, in fact, drizzling.

Although the places through which I was passing were familiar, I was still unable to recognise them. I felt lost, I didn't know where I was, perhaps because from my street-level perspective I could only see the ground floors of all the buildings, so that I couldn't quite identify them, although that stopped bothering me once I started to entertain myself by speculating on the height of those buildings.

To some extent I was making this journey with great expectations after so many months of misanthropy, but I found it difficult to accept that something I thought I knew well should have changed so much. And all of a sudden, as I was looking through the car window with the greatest curiosity, I understood that what I was able to see corresponded to what in reality had always been my usual perspective, as if I had always travelled around Barcelona at street level. Then it started to rain harder, and, a second later, through the window I recognised, with an unexpectedly strong emotion, the base of the Columbus Monument. There are no other cities, Mandiargues wrote in *The Margin*, like Barcelona, where the statues are placed so high, as if those in charge were afraid to place them within people's reach. Not knowing what to do with a sudden vision of this nature, I acted like a tourist in my own city and, using the camera on my phone, I took a photograph of the nondescript base of the invisible monument together with the curtain of rain that shrouded it. ✈

ENRIQUE VILA-MATAS was born in Barcelona, where he still lives. Considered one of Spain's greatest living writers, he is the author of a vast, provocative and highly personal body of work that includes novels, short stories, articles and essays. His work has been translated into twenty-nine languages and has attracted numerous awards in Spain, France, Portugal, Italy, Venezuela, Chile and Mexico, and he has been created a Knight of the French Legion of Honour. His English editions include *Bartleby & Co.* (2004), *Never Any End to Paris* (2011), *Dublinesque* (2012) and, most recently, *Mac's Problem* (2019), aka *Mac and His Problem*. The first text included here, 'La Calle Rimbaud', dates from 1995 and was originally published in the collection of essays *El Traje de los Domingos*, while the second, 'Barcelona, Flowing Down to the Sea', was written in 2022 for the Spanish literary magazine *Quimera*.

Catalonia:
A European History

Barcelona was the main stage for the renewed conflict between the Catalan government and the central Spanish authorities that culminated in the unrecognised referendum of 1 October 2017, which led to scenes of violence and convictions for 'sedition', an unimaginable turn of events in a 21st-century liberal democracy. To understand how this came about, you have to look at the history of Catalonia – and to overcome the current deadlock, it might just be necessary to rethink the very idea of the nation state.

PERE ALMEDA I SAMARANCH
Translated by Tiago Miller

A member of the Meridiana Resisteix collective, who gather every day in Sant Andreu to demonstrate for Catalan independence.

Barcelona is one of the most admired cities in the world, and the Catalan capital continues to be one of the most popular places to visit and to live, having been listed for decades at the top of world-city rankings. Reasons are not in short supply: a vibrant cultural scene, fascinating urbanism and architecture, social cohesion, quality of life and economic and industrial dynamism. But the global attraction that Barcelona has generated as a cosmopolitan Mediterranean city, with its own distinct culture and traditions, cannot be understood without first understanding Catalonia.

Barcelona is the administrative centre, capital city and 'heart and soul' of Catalonia, itself a European nation with hundreds of years of history. It is a country nestling against the Mediterranean Sea, crowned by the Pyrenees and not only a land link between the Iberian Peninsula and the European continent but also a land of miscegenation and refuge. Over the centuries its geographical location has enabled constant cultural and commercial exchange between north and south in a dynamic that has constantly evolved over time to shape its contemporary character. Catalonia's identity has been woven by these threads of tension and embellished by diverse influences, allowing it to forge a personality as an open, communicative society with its own history and a firm desire to project itself into the future.

Looking back at its past, however briefly, we find that we must search for its political origins in the 8th century, when the Frankish Carolingian Empire spread across half of Europe. This was a period in which the Hispanic March acted as a military buffer zone for the Carolingian Empire, a zone comprised of various counties along the Pyrenees and down to the sea, which included a large part of what today forms modern Catalonia. By the 10th century Catalan noblemen had already cut their ties with the Frankish kings and thus ushered in a new independent, sovereign era while also extending their territories south into those previously under the dominion of the Saracens. It is in the 12th century where we find the first evidence of the Catalan language in legal and religious texts, a language that has since enjoyed nine centuries of uninterrupted existence and which is one of the most prized features of Catalonia's identity.

The dynastic union between Catalonia and Aragon also took place in the 12th century. Although the union did not lead to a political merger – each territory maintaining its own laws and institutions – they did come together under the same crown to compose a proto-federation that still pervades the Catalan political and legal tradition. In the 13th century the Catalan-Aragonese crown expanded through the conquest of new territories in the kingdoms of Mallorca and Valencia, and later its dominions gradually spread

PERE ALMEDA I SAMARANCH is a lawyer and political scientist who, since 2021, has been director of the Institut Ramon Llull, the body that promotes the Catalan language and culture internationally. He is associate professor of political science at the University of Barcelona and has worked in several Catalan and international institutions as an expert in international relations, public policy and cultural management. He edited the volume *Catalunya-Espanya: Del Conflicte al Diàleg Polític?* (Los Libros de la Catarata, 2021), one of the reference texts for a recent analysis of the state of negotiations between Barcelona and Madrid to which about sixty authors contributed.

Catalan is a Romance language with around ten million speakers. It enjoys differing levels of official status in Catalonia, the Balearic Islands, the Community of Valencia, Andorra, the east of Aragon and in Alghero, Sardinia; on the other hand, it enjoys little in the way of protection in Roussillon (France) or El Carche (Murcia). Although in all these areas almost the entire population will at least understand the language, on average fewer than half use it daily in every social situation. In Catalonia it is the habitual language of communication of around 40 per cent of inhabitants, although in general, in the large urban centres such as Barcelona, Valencia or Palma, Spanish dominates. Outside of Spain, in Alghero and in Roussillon, Catalan is struggling; on the other hand, it is the only official language in Andorra and can therefore be used in the UN General Assembly. The invasive presence of Spanish has ensured that spoken Catalan contains a wealth of lexical borrowings and expressions that have altered under the influence of Spanish – people often use the term *Catanyol* (a hybrid of **Català** and Espa**nyol**, i.e. Catalanish) to refer to Catalan spoken in the streets. Nevertheless, the language is in good health. In Catalonia, it is the only language of instruction in state schools. There are numerous radio and TV broadcasters, newspapers and magazines as well as music, film and theatre productions in Catalan. It is used in politics, for religious purposes and in public administration. The book publishing sector is also buoyant, and all the international classics and bestsellers are translated into the language. Two academies (the Institut d'Estudis Catalans and the Acadèmia Valenciana de la Llengua) are responsible for standardisation, while the Institut Ramon Llull promotes Catalan language and culture abroad. (S.B.)

across the Mediterranean to Sardinia, Naples and (owing to the establishment of the Great Catalan Company and the mobilisation of the fearsome Almogavar warriors) as far afield as the duchies of Athens and Neopatras. It was then that the four great chronicles of the Aragonese kings and Catalan counts (collected as the *Crónica Pinatense*) were written, which relate, from the perspective of those in power, the principal events of the time. As a collection, these documents represent one of the most important historiographical texts of the entire medieval period, a time that also saw the publication of some of the most valuable works of Catalan literature, including the philosophical essays of Ramon Llull and Joanot Martorell's lengthy chivalric romance *Tirant lo Blanc*.

Between the 13th and 14th centuries one of the leading institutions of the Catalan political system – and one of the oldest in Europe – was established, the Generalitat, or General Council. Its founding was the result of a long dialogic tradition according to which a sovereign was not permitted either to enact constitutions or laws or demand taxes without the authorisation of the Corts, a parliament represented by the territory's three principle 'arms': the military, the ecclesiastic and the royal. The Corts Catalanes represented parliamentary negotiation between the monarch and the different arms of society to agree upon new laws of governance, manage damages and complaints and set the contributions that were to be received by the crown. The Generalitat had the role of acting upon these decisions, which were mainly fiscal in nature. Its headquarters were established in the houses along Carrer de Sant Honorat, forming the nucleus of the beginnings of the Palau de la Generalitat, which is where the Catalan government still sits some seven centuries

'Power in Barcelona has been concentrated in the same part of the city for almost two thousand years.'

later. In fact, power in Barcelona has been concentrated around Tàber hill, right next to the Temple of Augustus that dominated the 1st-century Roman colony of Barcino, for almost two thousand years.

Towards the end of the 15th century the dynastic union between the head of the Catalan-Aragonese monarchy, King Ferdinand II, and Queen Isabella I of Castile (the two later known as the 'Catholic Kings') marked the beginning of the modern era and sealed Catalonia's fate over the following centuries. A period of instability between the two territories unfolded, leading to growing tension between Catalan institutions and royal power. As a result, numerous conflicts took place between the 16th and 18th centuries, the most notable of which was the Reapers' War of 1640–52, a conflict on a European scale that would lead to heavy losses on the Catalan side after it rose up in arms in protest at abuses by Castilian troops still involved in the Thirty Years War against the French monarchy. It was within the vicissitudes of this conflict that Catalonia dissociated itself from the Spanish monarchy and briefly joined the French crown. Nevertheless, after the Treaty of the Pyrenees brought an end to the war, Catalonia ended up losing one-fifth of its territory and a substantial part of its population after Spain sacrificed the northern Catalan counties and handed them over to France. This period of European warfare culminated in the Peace of Westphalia (1648) and the subsequent redrawing of the continent's national borders. At the beginning of the 18th century the death of Charles II of Spain without an heir led to a power vacuum that resulted in the War of the Spanish Succession (1701–14) over the control of the vacant throne. The contenders were the Habsburg dynasty, which received support from Catalonia, and the Bourbon dynasty, backed by Castile. The conflict also had a clear geopolitical character, but it would gradually leave Catalonia isolated from other European powers and without allies in the defence of its preferred pretender. The war would end in favour of the Bourbons and Philip V. Years later Voltaire, one of the leading writers and philosophers of the Enlightenment, would reflect lucidly on these historical events in his work *The Age of Louis XIV*, in which he refers to Catalonia as 'one of the most fertile lands on earth yet one of the most unfortunately situated'. He goes on to affirm that 'despite the Catalan people's extreme love of liberty, they have been subjugated throughout their entire history', before stating that 'Catalonia can do without the world, but its neighbours cannot do without her.'

Perhaps the historical moment of greatest significance after the War of the Spanish Succession was the destruction of Barcelona on the 11 September 1714 following a merciless, fourteen-month siege by Bourbon troops. Not long after the capital's fall, King Philip V proclaimed his right of conquest and – desperate to punish the vanquished even more – enacted the Decrets de Nova Planta, a series of decrees that abolished Catalan institutions and their legal frameworks and subsequently concentrated complete power in the hands of the newly established absolutist monarchy. In one fell

Antoni Gaudí's La Pedrera, photographed on la Diada de Sant Jordi, 23 April.

swoop, the joint monarchy was swept aside and a unified, centralised monarchic model, based on the laws of Castile, was installed. This model had little respect for Catalonia's laws and juridical tradition. What's more, this latest defeat was accompanied by a new attempt to impose Castilian culture, politics and language. Nevertheless, the defeat of 1714 gained new historical significance as a symbol of Catalonia's resistance in the face of repeated attempts by the Spanish crown to wipe out its institutions. Since the 19th century Catalans have commemorated 11 September as an opportunity to assert their claim to self-governance and political and linguistic freedom. After the return to democracy in Spain after the death of Franco the day was made an official public holiday, known as the Diada Nacional de Catalunya, and it retains its political connotations.

*

In the mid-19th century, after a long period of economic and political decadence, Catalonia was given a new lease of life during an era of rapid industrialisation driven by steam energy, greater economic integration with the rest of the peninsula and growing trade abroad. During this time Barcelona underwent a transformation. After decades of demands and moves in favour of tearing down the old medieval walls as well as rising tensions with Madrid – which wanted to prevent this from going ahead – the Pla Cerdà, a plan that would allow the city to be greatly enlarged thanks to the construction of the Eixample residential area, was approved. Simultaneously, an artistic and intellectual movement focused on cultural revival began to flourish. Known as la Renaixença (the Renaissance), this movement aimed to renew and bestow prestige on Catalan

language and culture. These cultural ambitions were paired with the resurgence of a strong collective consciousness and identity regarding Catalan nationhood, resulting in the appearance of Catalanism as a transversal social movement that claimed Catalonia's right to exist as an independent political entity. Catalanism as a political and ideological movement was based on various traditions, mainly popular republicanism and federalism, but it must also be understood within the context of an era of emerging nation states across Europe. Nevertheless, its cultural, linguistic and political assertions were met (and are still being met) with obstacles and restraints imposed by a Spanish power system structured on a Castilian national model under the yoke of a political elite dominated by the Catholic Church, a decadent aristocracy and branches of the military linked to rich landowners always willing to threaten to rise up in arms against a precarious constitutional system that itself never culminated in revolution or the enactment of pending liberal reforms.

The beginning of the 20th century saw political Catalanism in full swing. On the cultural level, *modernisme* (Catalan modernism) and then *noucentisme* became central to all of the era's most salient debates. Despite their tension and opposing symbolisms, both developed into revolutionary movements very much in the spirit of the times, whether in the aesthetic fields of art and architecture or those of literature and philosophy. *Noucentisme* in particular was responsible for driving a civic, social and cultural meditation, yet with very real ambitions to interrupt and transform the reality of the time. Linked to other major contemporary European trends, it actively promoted a programme of political regeneration that pervaded

Right and below: Girls and boys in traditional costume before a dance performance.

the nascent Catalanism. New political organisations and new leaders appeared, who would participate in the incipient Spanish liberal representative system before the Mancomunitat was established in 1914. This new institution grouped the four Catalan provincial governments together into one council and saw them act on territorial issues in Catalonia for the first time since 1714. Despite its initial limitations, the Mancomunitat was able to enact a series of policies that included developing necessary infrastructure, constructing the Barcelona Metro system and initiating the creation of basic services aimed at modernising the country. These were years of economic prosperity strengthened by a non-intervention policy during the First World War, alongside the fact that Catalonia was able to attract a significant level of migration:

Since 2010 the Centre d'Estudis d'Opinió (CEO), under the direct control of the presidency of the Generalitat, has undertaken surveys of public sentiments on independence.

Do Catalans have the right to decide their own future through a referendum?

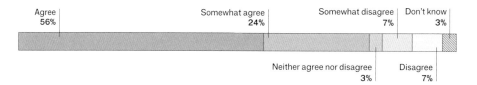

| Agree 56% | Somewhat agree 24% | Somewhat disagree 7% | Don't know 3% |
| | Neither agree nor disagree 3% | Disagree 7% | |

What type of political entity should Catalonia be in relation to Spain?

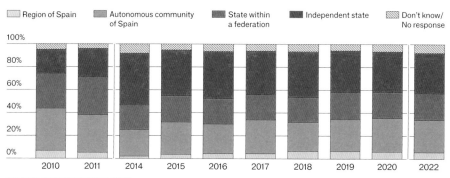

Region of Spain / Autonomous community of Spain / State within a federation / Independent state / Don't know/No response

SOURCE: CEO BAROMETER, 2022

thousands of people arrived there from the rest of Spain (notably Murcia and the south) in search of new economic opportunities within Catalan cities and their growing industries. Indeed, Catalonia's population increased by 20 per cent over the following decades, with these new arrivals becoming integrated into the social and political dynamics of the era. It was also during the first decades of the 20th century that the labour movement in Catalonia became increasingly strong, expressing itself through Marxist and socialist unions and organisations highly influenced by anarchist and libertarian thought. A popular social seed would flourish in diverse forms among the proletariat, including fraternities, mutual-aid groups and cultural centres that would offer social, educational and cultural assistance to the working classes. In 1910 the CNT (Confederació Nacional del Treball) was founded in Barcelona, and this anarchist union would go on to boast almost a million members by the end of the decade, wielding considerable power across Catalonia and the rest of Spain.

However, just when it seemed that

Catalanism and self-government was beginning to consolidate, yet another military coup took place in Spain. Driven by growing social tensions and supported by the aristocracy, the Primo de Rivera dictatorship took power in 1921; this was, in essence, a reactionary response to increasing antipathy over structural inequality in Spain, the failures of colonial policies and growing Catalan demands. In keeping with the absolutist tradition, the Rivera dictatorship dissolved Catalan institutions, suppressed Catalan republicanism and halted the modernising efforts that were beginning to bear fruit. Nevertheless, the dictatorship quickly became unpopular, and only a few years later lost all prestige, leaving it without social or political backing. Opposition forces grouped together under the Pact of San Sebastián, forcing the regime's ultimate fall, and in the resulting municipal elections of April 1931 republicanism clinched a historic victory across Spain, forcing King Alfonso XIII to flee the country.

On the 14 April 1931 Francesc Macià – the charismatic septuagenarian leader who had brought Catalanism and Catalan republicanism together – emerged on to the balcony of the Generalitat on Plaça de Sant Jaume in central Barcelona to proclaim the Catalan Republic a 'constituent state of the Iberian Federation', thus beating the declaration of the Second Spanish Republic in Madrid by a few hours. His speech pushed tensions to the limit within the nascent republican movement and led the recently formed Catalan and Spanish governments to agree just a few days later to name the new Catalan government after its old medieval institution: la Generalitat de Catalunya. Thus began a period of hope, which represented an important step forward in advancing the social and democratic reforms that had been pending

for decades. Principally, these included the territorial question and the recognition of Catalonia's right to self-government as enshrined in the Statute of Autonomy of 1932. However, the period proved not only to be decidedly short but also very tense because of the constant sabotage by reactionary forces and the ascendency of fascism across the continent of Europe. In Spain this meant organised opposition to any form of social progress and a violent belligerence towards the entire notion of Catalanism. These groups put their faith in a centralised model that excluded any identity that was not overtly Spanish and Castilian, and the tension finally erupted in the military uprising by General Franco and his fascist troops against the Republic, resulting in the Spanish Civil War of 1936–9, a bloody prelude to the Second World War. Nationalist victory and the establishment of the Franco dictatorship automatically led to the suppression of Catalan institutions and autonomy in a cruel reminder that history, if left unchecked, is doomed to repeat itself. An era of violent repression and persecution of Catalanism and Catalan culture began. The Catalan language was outlawed in public spaces, including churches, the president of the Republican Generalitat, Lluís Companys, was deported from France by the Nazis, given a show trial and summarily executed by a firing squad at Montjuïc Castle in 1940 and thousands of Catalans were executed or imprisoned after the Civil War, when it is estimated that the Republican exodus amounted to more than half a million people.

The years that followed were brutal, and it was not until the 1950s that the terrible economic situation showed any signs of improvement and the regime's development plans began to take effect. The economic progress of Catalonia was accompanied by a new wave of immigration

Politics in Catalonia

The main political parties
and where they stand on independence

SIMONE BERTELEGNI
Translated by Alan Thawley

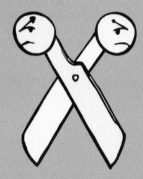

Junts per Catalunya
JxCat (Together for Catalonia)

A sort of evolving political chimera, founded
in 2018 by the former president of the
Generalitat, Carles Puigdemont, the JxCat
is pro-independence but has no specific
political orientation. In theory, the lion's share
of its votes come from former supporters of
Convergència Democràtica de Catalunya
(CDC), the longstanding pro-autonomy,
centre-right party that it eliminated from the
Catalan Parliament, but it also absorbed a
number of smaller parties, associations and
individual politicians, some of them from
the left. The old CDC was the party of Jordi
Pujol, the Catalan nationalist and opponent
of Franco once venerated as the father of
Catalan autonomy but whose reputation
was trashed in the most banal of ways,
when he admitted to having money stashed
in foreign bank accounts. In Madrid, King
Juan Carlos was at the centre of a scandal,
while in Barcelona, it was 'King' Jordi – and
they say the two cities are so different ...

Esquerra Republicana de Catalunya
ERC (Republican Left of Catalonia)

A historic independence party (once led by
Francesc Macià and Lluís Companys), the ERC
is the only Catalan nationalist party that fields
candidates in almost all Catalan-speaking
areas. Although its results are markedly worse
than in Catalonia, it crops up on ballot papers
in the Balearic Islands, the Community of
Valencia, eastern Aragon and even Roussillon
in France. Its leader, Oriol Junqueras (who
served time in prison following events linked
to the 2017 independence referendum),
studied at the Italian high school in Barcelona
so as not to attend an establishment linked
to the Franco regime, and he has always
chosen to speak in Italian in the European
Parliament in order to avoid using Spanish.

Partit dels Socialistes de Catalunya
PSC (The Socialists' Party of Catalonia)

A 'satellite' party of the Spanish Socialist
Workers' Party (PSOE) that describes itself as
federalist, regionalist as well as socialist, even
though it always gained the bulk of its votes
from southern-Spanish immigrants during the
economic boom years. Its stronghold lies in
the working-class outskirts of Barcelona and
areas outside the city, such as L'Hospitalet
de Llobregat, Catalonia's second-most
populous city, where, up until a few years ago,
it was a very rare thing to hear Catalan being
spoken. The majority of its votes now come
from the metropolitan area of Barcelona.

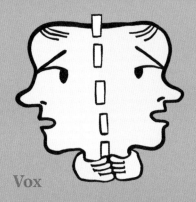

Vox

A newcomer to the Catalan Parliament, having burst on to the political scene in 2021, taking votes from the Partido Popular, which was evidently seen as not centralist enough. Vox is a party that makes few bones about its right-wing stance, having been established first and foremost to champion Spanish identity and to counter the regionalist parties (in Catalonia it has a fight on its hands) but is also vociferous in its defence of the traditional family, hunting and bullfighting.

Ciutadans
Cs (Citizens)

Founded by former swimming champion Albert Rivera, Ciutadans originated as an exclusively Catalan party but one strongly opposed to Catalan nationalism, although it describes itself as pro-autonomy (and liberal). In the elections immediately following the 'declaration of independence' it managed to catalyse the pro-Spanish vote, becoming the largest Catalan party. This success encouraged it to stand nationally as a centre-right alternative to the Partido Popular (PP), which was weakened by serious corruption scandals. However, the decision to give in and form governing coalitions with the PP in various places ended up eroding its electoral base.

Candidatura d'Unitat Popular
CUP (Popular Unity Candidacy)

A coalition of pro-independence, far-left, environmentalist and feminist groups, openly anti-capitalist and not exactly pro-Brussels. In theory, its politicians have no autonomy or room for manoeuvre, instead having to execute decisions taken via direct-democracy mechanisms involving all CUP activists.

En Comú Podem
ECP (Together We Can)

A far-left and environmentalist coalition, which also includes the Catalan branch of Podemos; if you were playing 'spot the difference' between the CUP and ECP, you could say that the latter does not describe itself as openly pro-independence but is instead in favour of a referendum to decide on the issue. ECP's greatest political triumph was undoubtedly winning the mayoral election in Barcelona with Ada Colau.

Partido Popular
PP (People's Party)

The party that has traditionally been one of the dominant forces at a national level needs little introduction. In the most recent Catalan elections, however, it almost failed to meet the electoral threshold. Its most charismatic figure is Xavier García Albiol, a towering former basketball player, as well as the first (and last) PP mayor of a major Catalan city (Badalona, 2011–15 and 2020–1).

from other parts of Spain, and in less than two decades almost a million people arrived, primarily from Andalusia. From the 1960s onwards repression relaxed, but political and social freedoms did not follow, meaning that Catalan democratic organisations were forced to pursue an underground resistance to the dictatorship. Nonetheless, the regime would survive until the dictator's death in 1975.

*

Franco's death ushered in the Transition, which was negotiated between the leaders of the Franco regime and the democratic parties, who accepted the monarchy imposed by Francoism in exchange for the evolution of the regime into a democratic parliamentary system. Passed in 1978, the Spanish Constitution was supposed to allow the nation to overcome forty years of Francoist dictatorship and resume the path towards becoming a liberal European democracy, while resolving the domestic problems stemming from Spain's territorial organisation, most notably the relationship between the Spanish state and Catalonia. Thus the agreements that would form the basis of the territorial system established in the constitution and developed by the autonomy statutes were devised to adapt to intense demands for self-government and national recognition, principally from Catalonia and the Basque Country.

Yet almost three decades later repeated failures to observe these agreements and the very principles that inspired the Transition's territorial pact, combined with the imbalance created by the Spanish state's recentralising actions, led slowly but surely to a rupture in relations. With its federalising ambitions, the new Statute of Autonomy of Catalonia of 2006 was an attempt to rebalance this loss of power and

FROM CATALONIA WITH LOVE

The story began with a van stopped by the Spanish police. It was full of documents belonging to their Catalan counterparts and heading for the incinerator. This was October 2017, in the days of the independence referendum, and investigations revealed that since at least 2014 the local Catalan police, controlled by the pro-independence autonomous government, had been running its own secret intelligence service – complete with moles and informants – to spy on Catalan lawyers, politicians, teachers and journalists deemed to be opponents of the 'Procés'. According to the separatists, however, the initial responsibility lay with the central government. An investigation run by the Catalan Parliament complained of a dirty war waged by Madrid's interior ministry since as far back as 2012 – stories leaked to the press to drag the pro-independence leaders through the mud and delegitimise the entire movement. The Spanish government denied the accusations, explaining that at the time the police were indeed investigating a number of Catalan politicians – but for corruption. In 2022 an international journalistic investigation into the Pegasus spyware developed by the Israeli firm NSO revealed that at least sixty-seven pro-independence activists and politicians, including four presidents of the autonomous government, had been targeted by surveillance ops. NSO insists that its spyware was sold exclusively to national governments, so suspicion fell on the Spanish secret services, whose reputation took another hit when it emerged that the telephones of the Spanish prime minister and other members of his government had been infected with Pegasus. But who was responsible? The spy war is another difficult chapter in the independence process; rebuilding mutual trust will not be easy.

authority after successive moves made by legal and political institutions in Madrid. But in 2010 came the Constitutional Court's shocking decision (despite a large number of its members' terms having expired) to amend or revoke the main articles from the statutory reforms that had been agreed between the Catalan and Spanish parliaments and ratified in a popular referendum. Consequently, the Spanish political system suffered a profound loss of legitimacy and credibility in addition to the disaffection of the social and political majority in Catalonia towards the centralised state and its institutions. This latest episode scuppered the expectations of those who, up until that point, still believed in the possibility of transforming Spain into a multinational state that respected Catalonia's identity and right to self-government. The sentence handed down by the Constitutional Court was taken as a democratic wrong, one that was very hard to justify, and it ended up lighting a political fuse that led to the growth of the independence movement. In the years that followed, mass protests took place on Catalonia's national day as part of an organised push for independence, with millions of people marching for their right to vote in a referendum on self-determination.

Those years were also witness to numerous official initiatives and proposals by the Catalan government to broker a deal over a legally binding referendum that were consistently rejected by the Spanish government and any further negotiation blocked. However, in 2014 a dress rehearsal took place through a non-binding consultation across the whole of Catalonia in which more than 2.3 million people voted, with 80.8 per cent voting in favour of independence. Years later this popular consultation would lead to Artur Mas,

then president of the Generalitat, being removed from office by the Spanish courts on charges of embezzlement of public funds. Parliamentary elections were called in Catalonia (with voter support), and the main pro-independence parties joined forces under the same banner, demanding a clear answer from the electorate on the question of independence: 47.8 per cent voted for pro-independence candidates, and 39.11 per cent voted for unionist candidates, while the rest favoured parties unwilling to take an explicit stance. Despite the pro-independence victory, the coalition fell short of the 50 per cent they had been seeking in order to justify continuing the process. This should have made parties of all political allegiances reconsider their strategies, but in reality it did little to stop the pro-independence rhetoric of a movement that was now seriously considering a binding referendum on self-determination before the term had expired.

The new Catalan government that was voted in decided on 1 October 2017 as the date for the referendum. As the day drew nearer, questions and doubts grew regarding exactly how the vote would go ahead, bearing in mind the pressure from Madrid, the legal barrage from the Spanish courts and the police operation under way to prevent any electoral activity. The referendum was suspended by the Constitutional Court and was actively opposed by the Spanish government, who sent more than ten thousand police officers to Catalonia. Nonetheless, the collaboration between the Catalan government and the main pro-independence groups, combined with an exceptional display of grassroots self-organisation, finally fooled the police units, while pro-independence voters mobilised en masse to occupy, open and later defend polling stations. The grotesque scenes of

The Catalonian separatist flag flying on a street in El Born.

Spanish police officers confiscating ballot boxes and voting slips, along with their indiscriminate, extreme violence against ordinary Catalans peacefully voting on the morning of 1 October, were seen all over the world, yet, despite state repression, the referendum went ahead. More than two million people voted (43 per cent of the electorate), while it is believed that 700,000 votes were confiscated by police officers. The result was resoundingly in favour of independence, with 90.18 per cent voting 'yes'. Those in favour of remaining part of Spain either abstained or actively boycotted the popular vote.

Despite the activist Julian Assange saying immediately after the events that 'whatever happens in Catalonia will set a precedent of either freedom or oppression for the entire world', the referendum failed to earn support from European institutions, and the international community did not recognise the result. Nevertheless, on 27 October the Catalan Parliament, in accordance with laws that it had previously passed, *symbolically* declared independence, but leaders were either unwilling or incapable of implementing it, and a gridlock was reached, thus provoking an enormous sense of disappointment among those who had voted. That same day the Spanish government suspended Catalan autonomy (history once again repeating itself) by enacting Article 155 of the Spanish Constitution, something that had never been used before, passed so that autonomous Catalan institutions would come directly under central government control. Unsurprisingly, snap elections were called. At the same time the judicial process began against leading figures in the Catalan government and the independence

In the ultra-polarised climate created by the Catalan independence process, both sides launched into rhetorical battles that reached dizzy heights of absurdity and tragedy, with reciprocal accusations of fascism and Nazism: claims that the Spanish government was a direct descendant of the Franco regime, or that the separatists were racists intent on promoting a sort of Catalan apartheid. In all this verbal violence, the worst insults were often directed at a group of people hated by all sides, the 'equidistants' or neutrals, who were accused of indifference, treachery or, worse, a naive indulgence that left them open to manipulation by the other side. In politics, Podemos and the coalition behind Ada Colau were able to negotiate this difficult path without declaring themselves either for or against independence but pushing for an agreed referendum. The attacks focused above all on intellectuals who advocated dialogue – from the film director Isabel Coixet, who had people shouting 'fascist' at her in the street, to the writer Javier Cercas, who defined Catalan separatism as 'a profoundly reactionary movement', or the TV presenter and comedian Jordi Évole, who found himself portrayed on a wanted poster as an 'equidistant' after daring to write in an article that 'in times of such certainty, confrontation and tension, doubt seems to me to be the last line of defence'. A few years since the peak of hostilities, and following the pardons granted by Spanish prime minister Pedro Sánchez to the separatists convicted for sedition, events today seem to be proving the equidistants right. Perhaps dialogue always was the best way forward.

movement, and those who were put on trial received long prison sentences for sedition, a crime better suited to the 19th century. Others, convinced of the repression that was coming, went into exile, one of whom was Carles Puigdemont, president of the Generalitat, who, to this day, still lives in Brussels where he actively denounces the conflict with Spain from his position in the European Parliament.

*

Without a shadow of a doubt, the autumn of 2017 marks a before-and-after watershed in relations between Catalonia and Spain, and six years later a satisfactory solution to the crisis is still not forthcoming. The establishment of ongoing dialogue and negotiations between both governments after Pedro Sánchez began his first term in office as prime minister of Spain represented an interesting terrain to explore, but, as yet, his government has shown no interest in collaborating nor has it put any proposals on the table beyond pardoning the imprisoned leaders – this is despite the constant demands from the Catalan side for real political talks.

Meanwhile the independence movement has entered a period of tactical redefinition and finds itself wrangling with deep disagreements over how to interpret everything that has happened, leading to contradictory positions over how to continue the process for national emancipation. The tactics adopted by the various political parties on how best to approach the present and future of Catalonia has as much to do with the constant fight for hegemony within a specific political space as it does with the internal logic of what is a transversal and ideologically plural movement. Nevertheless, now that the dust has settled after 2017, it is surely time to adopt a gradually more pragmatic

'There can be no pretence of neutrality in the positions that we adopt, just as there can be no neutrality in the words that we use to express ourselves.'

analysis both of the successes and mistakes of those years. A cold-headed look at the high-intensity politics of the time inevitably leads to the conclusion that the referendum of 1 October aimed to force Madrid into a corner and thus open up a new opportunity for real negotiation over Catalonia's future. Spain, historically averse to negotiations – which its political culture sees as a sign of weakness rather than an opportunity to avoid a more critical conflict – was plunged into one of the most serious constitutional and structural crises in recent European history. Likewise, the sense that Catalan leaders exhibited a certain naivety or miscalculation when gauging the Spanish state's capabilities and calibrating its possible response, together with (to their credit) their explicit position not to expose the population to a much more serious conflict, have generated a sense of frustration in Catalan society. However, the prevailing dissatisfaction has not demobilised the electorate, meaning that pro-independence parties still enjoy a parliamentary majority, albeit without the necessary political muscle to force the structural changes they desire.

In conclusion, explaining the political intensity experienced in Catalonia in recent years is not by any means a straightforward task, since it demands going beyond a mere description of events (difficult enough in itself) and providing an informed overview of their historical antecedents and contemporary evolution. Explaining it to international readers who lack the background knowledge brings with it the inevitable risk of simplifying or omitting the many nuances that shape our perspective. An array of emotions and tensions on both a collective and individual level have been experienced during the years in question, something that undoubtedly shapes our inclinations and prejudices when debating the subject. There can be no pretence of neutrality in the positions that we adopt, just as there can be no neutrality in the words that we use to express ourselves.

History shows us that this is a structural conflict that shapes both the Catalan and wider Spanish societies, one that has dragged on for centuries. Catalonia has had to survive within a nation state that has been its constant adversary, one that has historically fought against, suspended and abolished Catalan constitutions, its self-government and the laws that form its identity. During the 20th century successive Spanish authoritarian regimes acted without hesitation to destroy the very elements that form Catalonia. Democratic times have not been exempt from a deeply felt anti-Catalan sentiment rooted in the Spanish state's political culture, itself infused with an excluding Spanish nationalism. But, as we have noted above, periods of tension and popular revolt have also been a constant in the history of Catalonia. Protest has always been something that permeates its political culture and helps it to form its identity, whether a 15th-century peasant rebellion or the 20th-century *Setmana Tràgica* massacre of 1909. What is

surprising is that in the 21st century, within the framework of a democratic, liberal Europe, it's the same old story.

Obsessively chronicling the conflict causes a degradation both of public debate and our democratic institutions, but, above all, leads to the abandoning of numerous opportunities well within our reach if only we were capable of overcoming this centuries-old domestic conflict in accordance with the logic of the advanced democracy that we have within our collective grasp.

The political conflict between Catalonia and Spain is alive today and continues to be of unmistakable continental importance, given that it casts serious doubts over the nature of sovereignty within an EU member state. It is a conflict that must be reinterpreted within a redefinition of self-governance on a European and global level. There are many challenges that bring into question the role of nation states in the 21st century, and they have much to do with the range of issues that we must confront as a global community. What is more, the dynamics and evolution of an interconnected and interdependent world have shaped certain key concepts – such as sovereignty – that have been cornerstones of a foundational moment in modernity. We are only too aware of the need to press the reset button and rethink power structures in order to successfully meet our current needs head on. Without doubt, the pro-independence movement's greatest error was not daring to go beyond the concept of the nation state and obsessing over constructing one of its own rather than proposing other forms of government better suited to modern times. The nation state is no doubt an anachronistic political structure in many aspects, but it is still dominant in the 21st century. It is therefore within this framework, which is currently undergoing a paradigmatic shift as part of a constant transformation, that we need to interpret the conflict and Catalonia's demands. As a result, searching for a solution on a European scale that both normalises and articulates the democratic principle for these types of conflicts is essential. Political and territorial communities integrated into a nation state must have the right to assert themselves freely and to decide upon their political future beyond the narrow confines of current political systems. ✒

Barcelona, Festival City

The Catalan capital hosts two of the planet's best-known music mega-events: Primavera Sound and Sónar. This unique combination makes Barcelona the perfect context for a study of the impact of this type of event on the musical fabric of a city and on the lives of its residents – and, contrary to what one might expect, the impact is not a positive one.

NANDO CRUZ
Translated by Simon Deefholts

Chilling out on a slide in a public park on the way home after a messy night at Primavera Sound.

Barcelona has, historically, been a self-conscious city, and consequently it is a city historically obsessed with large-scale events. The Catalan capital has a long tradition of organising huge parties, attracting praise from abroad, that make the city's residents, business owners and institutions feel less 'second best' alongside actual European national capitals. Yes, in Barcelona we have a long-established inferiority complex that, although it has been gradually diminishing, actually made its first appearance (I'm not kidding) towards the end of the 19th century.

The 1888 Universal Exposition was the first mega-event that the Catalan capital used to give a boost to its individuality vis-à-vis its perennial rival, Madrid. An additional bonus was that Barcelona could present itself to the rest of Europe as a city with a fantastic range of cultural activities. Later there would be the 1929 Universal Exposition and, after the Franco era (a long period of darkness that is well known to all), Barcelona would host the mother of all mega-events, the Olympics, in 1992. Yes, this was a sporting rather than a cultural event, but it brought along with it the same processes: plans for urban regeneration, the construction of large facilities, gentrification, stunning cultural programmes, mass tourism and, ultimately, the international launch of the city's brand.

It may seem hard to believe, but in 1992 not a single music festival was held in Barcelona, nor even in the whole of Spain. At that time the vast majority of tours by international acts remained on the other side of the Pyrenees. All this would change, paradoxically, as a result of a major sporting event. And it would not happen gradually but overnight. In just five years Barcelona shook off its image as a provincial capital and took to the international stage as a European metropolis. For a sleight of hand of this type to work, it has to be done as quick as a flash – and by throwing money at it. That's what we're like in Barcelona. We might be the last to arrive at almost everything, but we'll catch up in no time.

YOU'VE GOT ONE? I'VE GOT THREE!
Glastonbury Festival, located in the English countryside more than two hundred kilometres from London, was the template for major festivals for several decades: a mass gathering in a rural setting, just like more short-lived events in the late 1960s, such as Woodstock, the original Isle of Wight and Monterey. Going to a festival was all about fleeing civilisation. It didn't make sense to organise a festival in a city. The big city meant parents, timetables, control, work, order ... Major festivals aspired to being the opposite: an escape from it all. Even today some large music events continue to offer a remote location as a key attraction. This is the format sold by one of the most famous festivals in the world currently, Coachella in California.

None of this means that there are no major music festivals located in big cities,

NANDO CRUZ is a music critic and journalist who has worked for television and radio as well as for various magazines and newspapers, contributing regularly to *El Diario*. Between 2016 and 2020 he wrote a series of articles on lesser-known music venues in Barcelona, 'Otros Escenarios Posibles' ('Other Possible Scenarios'), for *El Periódico de Catalunya*. He is the author of a number of music books, including a history of Spanish indie, *Pequeño Circo: Historia Oral del Indie en España* (Contra, 2015), and is currently working on a book about the impact of music festivals.

Born and raised in Sant Esteve Sesrovires, Catalonia, in 1992, Rosalía is, thanks to her second album, *El Mal Querer* (2018), an internationally renowned singer. Her first, *Los Ángeles* (2017), owed a great deal to the flamenco tradition; *El Mal Querer*, on the other hand, combined flamenco with R&B, while on its eleven tracks she reinterpreted the chapters of the *Romance of Flamenca*, the 13th-century literary text written in the Occitan language. The result has been described as 'complex' and not specifically designed to achieve global success, although that's what happened: the record, which began life as Rosalía's graduation project at the Catalonia School of Music, also earned her numerous awards. However, there was controversy, too: the singer was accused of cultural appropriation, because flamenco is a Roma musical genre, while some colleagues from the Latin American communities expressed their unhappiness at seeing a white woman with European roots triumphing at the Latin Grammy Awards. The singer responded to the criticism by asserting her right to use any style and any genre in total freedom, and, undaunted, on her 2022 record *Motomami* she mixes Dominican bachata with Korean and Japanese music, reggaeton with jazz and juxtaposes slow ballads with explicit lyrics. The record entered the charts in many European countries, cementing her status as a global pop star and an omnivorous and indefatigable talent. Musical creativity, according to Rosalía, comes from total anarchic freedom combined with the tireless work ethic of those who, like her, 'arrive first in the studio and are the last to leave'.

but it is without question less usual for a city to have two. Well, in Barcelona we have three. So there! The Sónar electronic music festival was founded in 1994, just after the big bang of the Olympics. A few months earlier there was also a short season of concerts by Spanish indie bands called Primavera Sound, which would not take its first steps towards becoming an international event until 2001. And in 2006, by which time these two festivals were firmly established and still expanding, a third emerged, Summercase, which, take note, was located at the same site to

'The cash just kept rolling in. Spain wanted to consolidate its place on the musicians' tour circuit, and the only way to achieve that (bearing in mind that record sales in Spain were always much lower than in the rest of Europe) was to pay whatever the foreign groups asked and add a bit more.'

which Primavera Sound had moved only the previous year to accommodate its now unstoppable growth: the Parc del Fòrum.

A DIGRESSION (WITH FIRING SQUADS)

Shall we have a quick word about the Parc del Fòrum? In the late 18th century Napoleon's troops would use the Camp de la Bota, an area on the outskirts of Barcelona alongside the river Besòs, as a place of execution by firing squad. By the early 20th century it had become a slum settlement for migrants from other regions of Spain, who had travelled to Barcelona to work on the construction sites for the 1929 Universal Exposition. Years later, at the end of the Civil War, precisely because it was a long way from the city centre, Camp de la Bota was chosen as the place for Franco's firing squads to execute more than 1,700 people. Towards the end of the 20th century the Parc del Fòrum was constructed here, an enormous expanse of concrete that would bury the memory of the victims of Francoism and which, from 2004 onwards, would accommodate all kinds of music events.

Barcelona's current festival venue was the icing on the cake for an urban development project that completed the transformation of a coastline, formerly plagued by shanty towns, into a recreational harbour with a zone of hotels and luxury apartments just a few metres away from the still-deprived neighbourhoods of Besòs and La Mina. It is no surprise that the implementation of these plans should come as a result of another great cultural event. But this time, since it was impossible to arrange a second Olympic Games or a third Universal Exposition, the Catalan capital came up with the Fòrum de les Cultures – a plethora of exhibitions, lectures and concerts commissioned thanks to a generous chequebook, with sustainability, peace and cultural diversity as its key features – to grace the umpteenth property speculation plan.

The following year, 2005, Primavera Sound moved to its new location in the Parc del Fòrum, as did Summercase in 2006. No one at that time could imagine that in 2008 the global economy would collapse. The cash just kept rolling in. Spain wanted to consolidate its place on the musicians' tour circuit, and the only way to achieve that (bearing in mind that record sales in Spain were always much lower than in the rest of Europe) was to pay whatever the foreign groups asked and add a bit more. Suddenly the big international agencies, who had never before picked up the phone to Spanish concert promoters, were delighted to bring their bands to Spain. Barcelona was their destination of choice: with three major festivals all bidding for the same groups (plus FIB in Benicàssim, 260 kilometres away), the asking price for their artists reached astronomical levels.

The figures didn't add up, because in Barcelona, however modern the city may aspire to be, there is not a large enough audience for indie music. But there's a local saying that goes, 'choose the largest donkey, whether or not it can walk', and when one of the donkeys stopped walking – Summercase went bust after its 2008 season – another festival took its place almost immediately. In 2010 the Cruïlla Festival booked the same dates in July and set up shop in the Parc del Fòrum. Barcelona had fully embraced the concept that was going to transform the live music industry: festival tourism.

If a foreign music lover is prepared to travel to Benicàssim and sleep in a tent, why would they not change their plans for a weekend in Barcelona, which also has sun, sea and sand, plus a very wide range of hotels and leisure activities on offer? Barcelona had its sights on the invention of the century: the urban mega-festival. So, if you can organise a mega-festival, why wait eighty years for the next Universal Exposition? And if you can put on three a year, why wait to be awarded another Olympic Games? All that was needed was to attract an international audience – and to lure them in, nothing better than to use the headline attraction for all the city's festivals: Barcelona itself.

In Spain there aren't so many people willing to pay two hundred euros for a festival ticket. People in this audience bracket tend to live in other countries, so the best strategy was to contact some leading foreign organisations and get them to curate some of the acts. The BBC in the UK, Radio Nova in France, the US digital magazine *Pitchfork*, the All Tomorrow's Parties Festival ... the line-ups for Sónar and Primavera Sound are organised directly or indirectly by the foreign media – whose global prestige draws in hordes of music lovers the world over – the same media that hardly deigns to give any thought to the tastes of the local audience. In this way, Barcelona's major festivals were gradually converted into resorts for music tourism aimed at foreigners.

The result: for years, at least 50 per cent of those attending Sónar and Primavera Sound have not been Spanish. If we deduct the numbers coming from other parts of Spain, the number of locals going to these festivals is alarmingly low. After an initial phase in which it desperately sought an international audience, the strategy adopted by the city's third largest event, the Cruïlla Festival, has been to focus on attracting a local crowd, and not necessarily dedicated only to indie or the latest movements. It is the only major music festival that can be called *local*.

A LABORATORY FOR 'FESTIVALITIS'

Barcelona has unwittingly become a laboratory in which the impact that major urban festivals might have on their surroundings can be studied. And the first and most obvious effect is a double-edged sword. The sudden interest in Barcelona on the part of booking agents for international artists soon became qualified: they were delighted to do business with Barcelona but mainly with the festivals, because they have the deepest pockets and attract the largest audiences. However, as a consequence the European festival capital has also become one of the cities with the poorest showing of indoor concerts.

For years many bands' European tours have not included dates in the Catalan capital unless it is to perform at a festival.

Left: Leaving the festival.
Above: Night revellers waiting for the tram
home after an all-nighter at Primavera Sound.

There are a number reasons for this, but all of them are rooted in the disproportionate status that festivals have acquired in the local diary. Festivals offer infinitely larger fees than a concert hall can afford, so the latter are not able to bid effectively for international tours. In addition, most festivals protect themselves with exclusivity clauses preventing the most highly valued artists in their line-ups from performing in the city for up to a year before and/or after the festival, in effect paying the bands a small fortune *not* to perform in the country for the rest of the year. And bands quickly get the message: you can earn more in just one night than you could in ten days on tour.

The Barcelona public, after years of these festivals, has also taken on board that the only solution is to spend two or three hundred euros and, in one weekend, see dozens of groups who might never pass through the city again. As a consequence, between May and July it's entrepreneurial suicide for any promoter to announce a performance in the Catalan capital. In fact, it's becoming more common to see tours with concerts in other Spanish cities but none of them coming to Barcelona. When a major festival bids for one of these bands at the price levels set by the international agents, the local market becomes completely distorted, and a slow and implacable process of desertification of the concert-hall circuit begins, at least when it comes to the genres that major festivals tend to feature.

And that is not all. These mega-events have such a wide reach that when the festival season arrives a large number of people working in the sector (sound and lighting technicians, stage hands, stage managers, runners and every type of assistant) take a break from their regular jobs (which are usually precarious) in order to shore up the machinery of the big festivals. Even young concert promoters who are trying to gain a toehold in a city with such powerful musical events have to realise sooner or later that placing their artist in a major festival will enable them to face the rest of the year with greater financial security. Some even end up working for the major festivals on a regular basis, which guarantees a youthful nose for fresh talent and excludes potential future competitors. For these and other reasons, major festivals function like black holes: they attract, spin, pulverise and swallow everything that comes within their orbit until almost nothing remains anywhere nearby.

A BLACK HOLE

But the effects of a major festival on a city go beyond the strictly musical. It is not just that they inflate market prices, distort the musical ecosystem, desertify the local cultural setup and mop up all the labour in the sector; they also have an effect upon the agendas of the news outlets, which, for weeks if not months at a time, live and breathe exclusively for the major festivals – in much the same way that political news is monopolised by the interests of political parties during an election – making the rest of the musical happenings in the city invisible by force of omission. And they also destroy the local government's cultural policies, since tens of thousands of euros will be allocated to subsidise these huge companies; tens of thousands of euros that, as a consequence, will never reach the precarious network of venues, agents and collectives that make up the fabric of Barcelona's grass roots.

Because underground and local neighbourhood music circuits do exist in Barcelona. There are hundreds of venues in this city putting on live music. Some

'Festivals also destroy the local government's cultural policies, since tens of thousands of euros will be allocated to subsidise these huge companies; tens of thousands of euros that will never reach the precarious network of venues, agents and collectives that make up the fabric of Barcelona's grass roots.'

of them seven days a week. Some of them two gigs a day. Some of them are small venues that, collectively, guarantee access to music at affordable prices throughout every district of the city and with a diverse mix of musical genres. In contrast, the large-scale music events are targeted at a section of the public with medium-to-high spending power; this is clear from both the ticket prices and the cost of food and drink sold at the venues, as well as their sponsors' advertising campaigns. And the financial favours that they receive from local government only serve to accentuate the culture gap in the population of Barcelona, encouraging and facilitating this type of event attended by an audience profile whose cultural needs are already serviced the rest of the year, while other sections of the population without regular access to culture remain on the margins.

Something else unusual has happened, precisely in Barcelona, where the business of festivals has grown and evolved at a supersonic pace. Two of the major festivals, Sónar and Primavera Sound, have sold a significant percentage of their shares to US investment funds, the former to Providence Equity and the latter to the Yucaipa Companies. The amount paid for these shares (a secret) represents one of the most obvious transfers of public funds to private hands ever

seen. All the subsidies and grants that the various local governments provided so that these private companies could grow and acquire international status have served, ultimately, to increase the price of their shares. And that is how these two flagships for the festival city have come to form part of the investment portfolios of companies located thousands of kilometres from Barcelona.

But there's no need to tear one's hair out. A major festival is, essentially, a mechanism to transform cultural capital into cash, a pop version of the tourist industry. The problem is that this cash is not reinvested in the cultural sector. The principal beneficiaries of staging a festival are the hotel and catering sectors; these businesses have nothing to do with music, but they get rich as a result of musical activity. An urban music festival is a mining agent that profits from the infrastructures, communications networks, public services and the city's symbolic capital (all of which assets are financed by taxes on the city's residents) and in exchange provides employment (usually poorly paid) and wealth ... but only for part of the commercial sector.

It can be seen very clearly in Barcelona that the major festivals are bubbles of turbocharged consumerism that barely permeate through to the surrounding

The pairing of paella and sangria, enjoyed in one of the many little waterfront restaurants in Barceloneta, is part and parcel of a typical weekend in Barcelona – regardless of the fact that locals look down on the combination with the same horror that Italians feel at the idea of pineapple on pizza. Food is an important part of the city's branding – you just need to look at the throngs of tourists at the *jamón* and cheese stalls at La Boqueria, the historic covered market on La Rambla – and the rich Catalan gastronomic tradition, based on tomatoes, peppers, garlic, olives and inexpensive fish such as sardines, anchovies and salt cod, lends itself to quick, informal meals with, why not, a seaview thrown in for good measure. Even El Bulli – the restaurant run by Catalan chef Ferran Adrià that was voted the best in the world several times before it closed in 2011 – started life as an informal seaside bar, a *chiringuito*, near Roses on the Costa Brava. Catalonia boasts three of the world's fifty best restaurants and a total of sixty-four Michelin stars – Barcelona alone has twenty-eight across eighteen restaurants, making it one of *the* top culinary destinations. But high-end cuisine is not the only game in town. The tapa most popular with tourists (and others) includes the extremely simple pa amb tomàquet, toasted bread rubbed with garlic and tomato, and many bars serve aperitifs with accompaniments based on tinned fish and seafood. Another 'humble' tradition is the *calçotada*, in which *calçots*, a kind of spring onion/scallion, are chargrilled in late winter, and the entertainment consists of getting your hands dirty dipping the onion in a special sauce made from tomato, roasted peppers, garlic, almonds and hazelnuts. And, in this case (*only* in this case), sangria really is a good accompaniment.

area. The Parc del Fòrum in which Primavera Sound and dozens of other major events with similar or large attendances take place, was built facing two of the most impoverished districts on the Barcelona coastline, Besòs and La Mina. Nothing has changed since then. The regeneration of an area by contagion is a fantasy. However, the shadow of gentrification looms so large that the festival itself could find itself hostage to new urban development projects in the vicinity that would make part of the land they currently occupy unusable. Capitalism is greedy and remorseless and never goes on a diet; tomorrow it could gorge itself on yesterday's best friend.

And then, of course, there's the question of the environment. At a time of climate crisis and attempts to control greenhouse-gas emissions, as fuel prices go through the roof and airline companies face financial meltdown, the very idea of organising cultural events that are only economically viable if they succeed in dragging hordes of foreign spectators across thousands of kilometres looks like ecological suicide. I repeat, there is no other city on the planet that receives more festival tourists than Barcelona. Add to that the numbers that come to watch Barça play and people looking for a weekend of beach, paella and Gaudí, and we're looking at a city on the brink of tourism-induced collapse. Tourism-phobia is a growing phenomenon in Barcelona, and the major festivals are in the firing line.

In the pressingly urgent debate on the 'touristification' of Barcelona, the major festivals are already seen as part of the problem rather than the solution. It's no accident that for many years the Association of Music Festivals has played a central role in FITUR, the most important tourism fair in Spain. The festival circuit

Above: A festival-goer rocked to sleep by the motion of the tram.
Below: Young men posing at the exit of Primavera Sound.

is one of the key drivers of tourism in our country, and Barcelona is one of its strategic sites. The Catalan entrepreneurs who in 1908 founded the Societat d'Atracció de Forasters (Society for the Attraction of Foreigners), an organisation promoting Barcelona as a tourist destination, would be astonished to see how, a century later, events apparently rooted in the counterculture, such as music festivals, have become trusted allies in the promotion of the Barcelona brand and in making ultra-consumerism seem cool.

If we take a look back, the Olympics and the Universal Expositions were even more crowded events, but they were one-offs. The big festivals, in contrast, attract smaller numbers, but they take place every year. In this respect they are more like trade fairs, events that guarantee tens of thousands of visitors year after year, generating a whole service industry around them. It is not by chance that Sónar, the only large festival that never wanted to move to the Parc del Fòrum, takes place in Gran Via, the venue that hosts the big trade fairs, from the Mobile World Congress to ISE (Integrated Systems Europe), which services the audiovisual sector, and not forgetting the International Boat Show and Alimentaria, the international food-and-drinks fair.

AND THEN CAME THE PANDEMIC ...
In 2020 there was only one festival in the whole world: the festival of best intentions. The pandemic came, and we threw ourselves into a collective examination of conscience. Do we have to learn to live with less? Is our pace of life inhumane? Will nature teach us the hard way what we refused to learn when the going was good? That summer the word 'downsizing' was on the tip of everyone's tongue. Even in Barcelona. Even in the music-festival

industry, which appeared to be in its death throes. The following summer Barcelona Province hosted three of the first major festivals allowed on the continent of Europe. The Cruïlla Festival brought together fifty thousand spectators while the fifth wave of the pandemic was raging, and with alarming levels of infection both in and outdoors and among health workers who were carrying out Covid tests. Although it is hard to believe, the health authorities did not dare cancel it. Such is the power that festivals have acquired in this corner of Europe.

The capitalist religion has only two commandments: 'Thou shalt love money above all things' and 'Thou shalt not downsize'. In 2022 the largest festival in Spain, Primavera Sound, has not downsized but has instead doubled its duration in order to recuperate the losses caused by two years of shutdown. It agreed with the city council that in 2022, on a one-off basis, the festival would last twelve days. But Primavera wants more; it wants to secure this two-weekend format indefinitely. It needs more income, and for that it needs to sell more tickets. And to sell more tickets it needs to sign up more bands and build more sets. And for that it needs a larger budget. And for that it needs more sponsors, more grants, more income. And for that it has to sell more tickets. And for that ...

A large festival is, by its very nature, an insatiable monster. The most difficult thing for a large music festival is not to define a brand, establish it in the market, maintain its appeal over time to recalibrate the age of its audiences; the most difficult thing is to understand when to stop growing. Sónar resolved this dilemma years ago by creating a three-day, two-night format that has, ever since, attracted crowds of around a hundred thousand. Meanwhile Primavera Sound

'A large festival is, by its very nature, an insatiable monster. The most difficult thing for a large music festival is not to define a brand, establish it in the market, maintain its appeal over time to recalibrate the age of its audiences; the most difficult thing is to understand when to stop growing.'

had grown so much that by 2010 the Parc del Fòrum was not big enough, and it started to expand both northwards and to the south, annexing another enormous sea of concrete popularly known as Mordor together with the neighbouring stretch of beach. The distance from one end of the enclosure to the other was two kilometres. Since 2017 Primavera Sound has attracted two hundred thousand festival-goers; following its double season in June 2022 the festival claims to have upped this to more than half a million.

Primavera Sound's exceptional attendance record was accompanied by records of another kind: hour-long queues for drinks, worrying collapses of the walkways between the various stages, a list of cancellations long enough to stage an alternative festival and an Instagram group with three thousand followers, christened Primavera Sucks, which served as a showcase for complaints, compensation claims and threatened reports to the authorities. A mantra throughout the festival was 'This is the last year I'll be coming'. For the first time the sense of extreme overcrowding has made a deeper impression than the artistic merits of the programme. Outside the enclosure, the problems caused by an event that brings together an average of eighty thousand people each day have also multiplied. Locals have formed a group called Stop Concerts to pressurise the city council into reducing the number of major events held at the Parc del Fòrum.

After two years of pandemic and the consequent festival blackout, 2022 has been a year of double or nothing. That's exactly how the director of Primavera Sound put it when he gave the city council a 'take-it-or-leave-it' demand typical of Barcelona entrepreneurs: accept our conditions or we'll move to Madrid. And their conditions were to establish the two-weekend festival format on a permanent basis. But when Primavera's threat arrived, the city council was already on a different page, debating crucial questions that no other European city has had to answer before but which have now become urgent for Barcelona. Is it culturally, financially and ecologically sustainable for a city to host three major festivals? What are the limits of a city's capacity as a location for cultural mega-events with global appeal? Who should be monitoring to ensure that those limits are not exceeded? What will be the reaction of the other major festivals to the fact that one of them has doubled in size? Are we at the dawn of a new era of *mega-mega-events*?

Barcelona has been divided on all this for some time. On the one hand, there are those who would like festivals to disappear from the city for ever; on the other, those

Above: What better way
to end a night at Primavera
Sound than with a dip
in the sea?
Below: The morning after
the night before.

It is difficult to separate the rise of Primavera Sound from the dominant role that has always been played by its director Gabi Ruiz. In 1994 the young promoter joined forces with an established figure in the sector, Serapi Soler, to launch the first edition. The partnership lasted just three years, but these were crucial years for the transition from a scene devoted only to indie music to the arrival of techno, which the pair championed with nights at the legendary club Nitsa, especially those put on by resident DJ Sideral. In spite of the successful formula, reportedly their personality differences became too great a strain, and Soler negotiated a payout worth 11 million pesetas (around $75,500), while Ruiz began to earn himself a name as a tough businessman who surrounded himself with flatterers. He reputedly carried on like this for years, weaving an increasingly complex web, amassing around him a clan of militant supporters (more than employees), who did not appreciate any competition, and, if they were unable to force their rivals out, would simply put them on the payroll. A case in point was the magazine *Rockdelux*, with which relations had been anything but good until it was absorbed to provide 'artistic consultancy' for Primavera. It is no secret that Ruiz does not like journalists, and those who dare to criticise him find themselves denied concert passes. To smooth over this abrasive, undiplomatic aspect of his personality, Ruiz found a partner who moves in high places, Pablo Soler, to deal with the venues and, if gossip is to be believed, to plug the holes in his finances. His critics say that through cronyism, lobbying, veiled threats and a meticulous campaign to buy up the best talents on the market, Ruiz has been able to rule the roost on the music scene through his record label, booking agency and as organiser of Primavera Sound.

who would be sorry to see Barcelona lose Primavera. But there is a third group, which is infinitely larger than the sum of the first two: those who have no idea what Primavera Sound has to offer because they will never have three hundred euros to spend on a music festival that has for years been growing behind its citizens' backs. In the end, on the final day of Primavera Sound 2022, its director announced that there will not be another two-weekend programme. Translation: the city council has not given in to the festival's expansionary aspirations. In 2023 Primavera will hold a one-weekend event in Barcelona and another in Madrid. And that is how things will proceed until at least 2027. 🐟

ALICIA KOPF

Translated by Kathryn Phillips-Miles

THE SEA AND ME:
A Conversation on Wheels

The pandemic encouraged Barcelona's residents to become more familiar with their city's beaches, often dismissed by locals as little more than tourist traps and largely avoided. Exploring Barceloneta on roller-skates, Alicia Kopf reflects on a city and seafront that seem to be designed solely from a male perspective.

The women of Rolling Retro
Barcelona before a skating
session.

I took my body anyplace with me.
In the thickets of abstraction my skin ran with blood.
From 'Lake Ghazal' by Adrienne Rich

It is impossible to look at a pair of roller-skates or a skateboard and not slip back into your childhood. This article, written on wheels, sprang from a desire to rediscover the pleasures of skating in one particular public space, the Barcelona seafront, with its unique characteristics, a place where the local Mediterranean culture, the financial elite and mass tourism all meet.

Learning how to skate again post-pandemic is a way of reclaiming my city's beach in a geography lesson on wheels. Because skating sharpens your feel for the asphalt, guiding you towards the smooth parts of the coastal avenues, and I glide under the shadow of giants. Between Barceloneta and Poblenou a number of buildings stand out: the Hotel Vela, the Mapfre Towers, Frank Gehry's 'Golden Fish', the Hotel Arts. A playful skyline full of vertical leaps and glittering metal, the most expensive – and also most controversial – post-Olympic array of jewels in the city.

If walking is reflective and conducive to thought, skating makes you laugh, causing the static to become dynamic and converting a thoroughfare into a play-ground. Leslie Kern, in her book *Feminist City* (Verso, 2021), reminds us that rather than starting with theory or policy or urban planning, we could begin with what the poet and essayist Adrienne Rich called the geography closest in, the body and everyday life. So, after two years of inter-mittent lockdowns I decide to rediscover, reappropriate and celebrate this coastline and this body, both of which belong to me and require sun.

In the absence of any other leisure activities that appeal to me in this area, I'm inspired – by some videos circu-lating on Instagram and by a friend who does a type of skating that originated in California in the 1970s called roller dance – to put my name down for some outdoor roller-skate dancing classes. Skating sports are usually characterised

ALICIA KOPF (the artistic name of Imma Ávalos Marqués) is a Catalan author and multi-disciplinary artist who has exhibited in major venues such as the Centre for Contemporary Culture and the Museum of Contemporary Art in Barcelona among others. Her first book, *Germà de Gel* (2015), published in English as *Brother in Ice* (And Other Stories, 2018), has received several international awards and been translated into nine languages. The book was the culmination of a cycle of several exhibitions entitled *Àrticantàrtic*. Currently she is working on the *Speculative Intimacy* exhibition cycle.

A young woman taking part in the Rolling Retro Barcelona classes led by Marcela Hattemer. In the background, Ricardo Bofill's iconic Hotel Vela, also known as W Barcelona.

'Keep calm and skate' must have been an idea that came to many people during the Covid restrictions: a liberating activity, something you can do in the open air while maintaining social distancing – and, if you happen to be sporty and photogenic, one that can earn you millions of hits on social media. So from the USA to Europe the rumour circulated that skates were back in style, hot on the heels of the scooter, their cousin in the sharing economy and another green and sustainable choice. But this supposed renaissance of a culture associated with the 1970s and 1980s – including the old-school quad skates with two pairs of wheels, one front and one back – is not without controversy, as there are those who consider it a form of cultural appropriation. In the African American community skates never went out of fashion, so there is a certain irritation at this 'rediscovery' driven by (mainly) white influencers. This is a sensitive area. Skating rinks were one of the last bastions of racial segregation in the USA – for many years Black people were denied access – but also one of the first places in which the protests emerged that led to the removal of prohibitions, although often the problem simply moved. The rules had changed, and Black people had every right to skate as well, but, in reality, segregation persisted, as rink-owners, who were almost always white, brought in separate evenings or venues for Black customers and whites. The African American skating (sub-) culture has also played a fundamental but perhaps overlooked role in the development of many musical genres, from funk to R&B and disco to hip-hop.

by hedonism rather than competitiveness, and if they incorporate rhythm and sunshine, it has to be the closest thing to happiness that I could wish for right now. I need flow, sea and levity.

The roller dance class takes place in a public park on the coastal avenue, out in the old – now gentrified – working-class district of Poblenou. At this point along the coastline the buildings are all new and very elegant, reflecting the sea with a certain serenity; there are no shops, and there are very few people to be seen in the garden areas between the blocks on the seafront. On this paved embankment beneath the palm trees we come across a group of women on quad skates (two wheels at the front and two at the back) wearing leggings, shorts and knee pads. It seems that this type of skate allows more movement than the more modern in-line variety, which are designed exclusively for the pace of city life and pure speed. The instructor places a nice-looking Marshall speaker on the ground, and we start to do circuits around a loop marked out with cones. The last time I did this same exercise with similar skates I was seven years old; later the fashion for in-line skates made me forget about quads. Gradually my body regains its muscle memory and recalibrates its centre of gravity in relation to my new prosthetic attachments, otherwise known as wheels. Rigoberta Bandini's 2021 release 'Ay Mamá' is playing from the speaker. The average age of our group – mainly women, although there are also one or two courageous lads – is somewhere between thirty and forty, all of us seeking to reclaim a dose of sun-inspired joy that the pandemic owes us. I realise that when it comes to the female body most activities that have to do with (sensual rather than sexual) pleasure take place in private spaces, indoors. Why should that be? Rigoberta Bandini's chorus plays full blast:

> *Mamá, mamá, mamá*
> *Let's make the city stop*
> *Exposing a breast*
> *Pure Delacroix-style*
> *Mamá, mamá, mamá*

Some thirty of us women are gyrating across the asphalt to the rhythm of the music. I imagine us all responding to the singer's proposal, and I laugh out loud. Why not? The beach is only a hundred metres away, and going topless there is quite normal. It's ridiculously easy to transgress the social code when you're treading the borders: that side yes, this side no. Show your breasts (over there) by all means, but in most places, no. *Ha!*

As we tour the loop, on one side of the horizon lies the luxurious W Barcelona Hotel and, on the other, the three chimneys of the now decommissioned Sant Adriá thermal power station on the banks of the Besós estuary. They bring back memories of an old and, dare I say it (to use a term I've just invented), *residual* relationship between Barcelona and its stretch of the ocean. And so I skate between two extremes of the Barcelona coastline, which are also socio-economic.

I keep coming back to the strange relationship between the city and the sea. Barcelona is a port city and, until the 1990s, it was an industrial city. The 1992 Olympic Games opened up the maritime horizon, envisioning a new relationship beyond using it for maritime commerce or for dumping waste. There is a clear example of the invisible frontier that the beach represents for a local person: for a Barcelonés, walking through the city in flip-flops and bathing trunks is considered the height of vulgarity, and, in fact, it is prohibited if the person concerned is also shirtless, something that has been known to happen with the advent of low-cost tourism. For this type of tourist, on the other hand, bearing in mind that the sea is so close, the beach extends to include the paved area. There is some logic to this, as they said in Paris in May '68: *Sous les pavés, la plage!* (Under the cobblestones lies the beach!)

For an ordinary Barcelonés the city does not have a coast; the beach starts to the north, beyond Blanes, and to the south it begins at Castelldefels. The sportier citizens, it's true, can enjoy the Barceloneta swimming club, making use of a swimming pool located alongside the sea. The local beach tends to be a last resort because it's so hostile, especially at night, with its frequent muggings and delinquent pigeons; just like the Ramblas,

A beach in the heart of the city is the dream for many an urban dweller, but those who have that luxury often end up looking for a nicer one, either because their local beach is overrun by tourists or because the water is filthy. Barcelona is no different, and in the summer locals leave the city's beach to the tourists and take the train along the coast. To the north, the railway line passes by a long series of large sandy beaches, from Badalona to Vilassar, which are too easily accessed from the city not to be full. After the town of Mataró the coastline gives way to beaches in little coves and villages where the bourgeoisie once built their summer villas, such as Blanes or Caldes d'Estrac, well known for its thermal spa in the early 20th century. To the south, the first stops are Gavà and Castelldefels, where many top footballers, including the likes of Messi, Suárez, Romário and Ronaldinho, have lived. The beach is a family destination, with an international flavour thanks to the proximity of the airport. In Garraf, a picturesque mountainside village, the atmosphere is more exclusive – the private club chain Soho House opened a branch on the beach in 2018. The most iconic location remains Sitges, a cultural and artistic centre since the late 19th century that had already become a 'miniature Ibiza' during the Franco era. It is also a historic LGBTQ+ destination, known for its beaches (including nudist beaches), night life and its film festival. The beach at El Prat de Llobregat, meanwhile, is only accessible by car and a stone's throw from the airport. It is not really a place for a swim – given that the water flowing from the port is not the cleanest – but it is a great place to enjoy some wilder surroundings, with its lagoons and pine woods that have been restored to health following the installation of a treatment plant on the river Llobregat.

we leave it to the tourists. Most of us avoid both places and await special measures to be implemented by the mayor. It appears that with regard to social mores on the beach, some initiatives such as banning smoking or closing down the more dubious night spots are starting to have an effect. We live in hope.

'Careful,' I tell myself as I continue to circle. I still lose my balance at times; you have to look ahead, bend your knees and keep your centre of gravity low. Everything in life is a question of identifying areas of support and spreading the weight, I tell myself, and I go around again. Rigoberta carries on singing:

> I don't know why people are so scared of
>   our tits
> Without them there'd be no human race
>   or beauty
> And you know full well
> Lo-lo-lo-lo-lo-lo-lo-lo-lo-lo-lo-lo-lo
> (You know full well)
> Listen to me
> Mamá, mamá, mamá

My attendance at these classes is inter-mittent; it depends on the weather (if it's not sunny, they tend to cancel them), and my availability at weekends is sporadic. I realise at the end of April that it's been months since I had a good look at myself. I took care of my physical needs, but I hadn't examined myself closely. I had been visited by Covid for the first time about a month before (fortunately a light dose), and that interrupted my wheeled acrobatic progress. I examine myself as I return from my forced hiatus; between my shorts and my knee pads I look paler, weaker, undepilated. No one notices; at this point in April most of us are in the same boat. I navigate the circuit calmly; you have to cross one foot in front of other

'A couple passes by with a large black dog that barks at us aggressively. His mistress says to him, "What's the matter? Don't you like women?"'

and twist your torso in order to turn. A couple passes by with a large black dog that barks at us aggressively. His mistress says to him, 'What's the matter? Don't you like women?'

If that question were directed at the city, feminist urbanism would reply that women have always been seen as a problem for the modern city. During the Industrial Revolution, the rapid growth of European cities produced a chaotic mix of social classes and immigrants in the streets. The social norms of the Victorian era included strict demarcations between the classes and a harsh code of etiquette designed to protect the purity of upper-class white women. The increasing urban contact between men and women and between women and the urban masses represented a rupture of this code. 'The gentleman and, worse still, the gentle-woman, were forced to rub shoulders with the lower orders and might be buffeted and pushed with little ceremony or deference,' writes the cultural historian Elizabeth Wilson in *The Sphinx in the City* (University of California Press, 1991).

In contrast to the typical *flâneur*, for a woman (especially once her early youth had passed and leaving aside the – still present – issues relating to her safety) to enjoy the urban space beyond merely passing through it traditionally carried an ideological risk in addition to the physical one: being considered an 'eccentric', a prostitute or someone outside the law, in other words, outside the patriarchal system, a person who lives by her own rules, who enjoys the city as an aesthetic experience, who is not concerned with anyone else unless she chooses to be. In other words, rather similar to a man. *Ha!*

The figure of the *flâneur* has been extensively revised by the feminist collective, starting with Lauren Elkin in *Flâneuse* or Leslie Kern herself in *Feminist City*: 'The figure of the *flâneur*, emerging prominently in Charles Baudelaire's writing, is the gentleman who is a "passionate spectator" of the city, seeking to "become one flesh with the crowd", at the centre of the action and yet invisible … as an essential urban character in the modern city, and urban sociologists such as Georg Simmel located traits like a "blasé attitude" and the ability to be anonymous as inherent to the new urban psychology. Not surprisingly, given the perspectives of these writers, the *flâneur* was always imagined as a man, not to mention one who is white and able-bodied.' Could the *flâneur* be a woman? Could this *flâneur* also bring a buggy for her baby? And what if she were on roller-skates? In urban feminist thought, some women saw the *flâneur* model as an exclusivist trope that had to be criticised; others, as a figure to be reclaimed. 'For those who reject the idea, women can never fully escape into invisibility because their gender marks them as objects of the male gaze. Others say the female *flâneur* has always existed. Calling her the *flâneuse*, these writers point to examples like Virginia Woolf.' That is what Kern argues. I laugh to myself again. I imagine myself skating and pushing a buggy, skating while holding my cat's lead. (My cat, confined

Opposite: Holding tight as the last rays of the sun go down; a man works out at Barceloneta's public open-air gym.
Above: Somorrostro Beach.
Left: A young woman working on her Sarvangasana with the Hotel Arts and the Mapfre Tower in the background.

to a small apartment, often begs me to take her out for a bit of a run.) Girls and women, young and old, skating. *Let's stop the city!* And I remind myself as well to inhabit our stretch of the sea.

I think of something that the American writer Rebecca Solnit once said about walking, and I look at my skates, which fascinate me because there is something a little childish in their roundness and colours and textures; perhaps what fascinates me is that they are designed for the enjoyment of an adult woman. I apply Rebecca Solnit's ideas to my new medium. What she said, in her book *Wanderlust: A History of Walking* (Penguin, 2001, USA / Granta, 2022, UK), was: 'Walking, ideally, is a state in which the mind, the body and the world are aligned, as though they were three characters finally in conversation together, three notes suddenly making a chord. Walking allows us to be in our bodies and in the world without being made busy by them. It leaves us free to think without being wholly lost in our thoughts.' Skating accelerates this process in the mind, the body and the world, making you aware of the city's texture. Its obstacles become challenges and opportunities to make a leap. This dialogue with architectural language is an act of rebellion against authority: to play with obstacles. It forces you to think out new strategies to be able to get past them. To go down a slope backwards.

Likewise, an extra element is added in relation to speed: their *flow* turns skaters – male and female – into skilful beings, as beautiful and fleeting as 'To a Passer-by' in Baudelaire's *The Flowers of Evil*.

The political repercussions of playfulness and happiness are strongest in joyful rather than angry protest. The levity of others irritates the establishment. The queer movement discovered this back in the 1980s and was able to take full advantage of the revolutionary potential of revelry in their parties and parades. And now these female roller-skaters meet up and demonstrate their moves in improvised roller disco sessions beneath the controversial, iconic Hotel Vela (so-called because it is shaped like a sail) or W Barcelona (its official name), a work by the recently deceased architect Ricardo Bofill. A controversial place because the construction of this hotel, the first to have direct access to the beach, breached the provisions of Spain's coastal-access laws and, according to the residents of Barceloneta, pushed up the cost of living in a traditionally working-class neighbourhood.

Mamá, mamá, mamá
Let's stop the city
Exposing a breast
Pure Delacroix-style
Mamá, mamá, mamá

Lockdown made me appreciate having a beach nearby, one I had previously ignored as being too touristy or focused on sports that were too expensive for the majority of locals to access. So, come to think of it, perhaps it was the beach that had been ignoring me, since I don't belong to any of the sports clubs or to the financial elite who seem to be welcomed by the port. After the 1992 Olympics the Olympic Port transformed an industrial city into a city open to the sea and to the rest of the world. It is not so unusual to live with one's back to the sea.

The beautification of the sea also has a history. The French historian Alain Corbin reveals in *The Lure of the Sea* that at the start of the so-called classical era in 15th-century Europe, a catastrophist theological vision of the sea and its shores was dominant in the minds of the old continent's popular masses. The ocean was feared like a remnant of the Flood and was not thought of as a place of recreation; rather than the edge of the land, coastlines were seen for centuries as the final extent of the sea. In other words, the beach was not a place of safety as a border of the land but rather an unsafe place as the boundary of an incomprehensible immensity. With the arrival first of the Renaissance and later of the modern era, two things emerge: a new naturalist theological vision (no longer catastrophist) and the appearance of the scientific vision. The natural theologians – in other words, the scientists of the era – struggled from around 1750 onwards to erase people's fear of natural phenomena, including the sea, and so, with the understanding of science, we learned to look at the sea with new eyes, those of the Romantics. But let's get back to the history of this beach.

This harbour, which embraces a small community of sailing-boat owners and numerous consumers of paella as well as accommodating fast-food enthusiasts, doesn't currently seem to offer any public activity in which I could participate, except for swimming in the municipal pool in an enclosed area. As for partying, until very recently the harbour's nightspots and the brawling among their clientele filled the pages of the sensationalist press, so local people tended not to go there for a drink. On a different note, somewhat healthier and out in the open air, we have volleyball, which is more in vogue with the expats than with the locals, although people are getting used to it, and my friends have gradually started giving it a go.

So what it comes down to is an urban dialogue about our beach, addressing a disparate and occasionally extremophile

GAYXAMPLE AND THE LGBTQ+ SCENE

As the third EU country to legalise same-sex marriage (in 2005), following the Netherlands and Belgium, Spain has long been at the forefront of LGBTQ+ rights. Over the years the country has passed numerous laws guaranteeing the queer communities, including non-binary and trans people, equal rights and protection against discrimination based on sexual orientation or gender identity, and Barcelona is one of the most popular destinations for tourists in search of somewhere gay-friendly. With its liberal atmosphere, lively nightlife and an inclusive community, it is home to the heart of Spanish LGBTQ+ life. This is particularly true of the Eixample neighbourhood, affectionately nicknamed Gayxample, where you can find queer beauty salons, bookshops, saunas, restaurants and sex shops, as well as numerous nightspots, including the popular Candy Darling – named after the transgender actress known for her work with Andy Warhol in the 1960s and 1970s – and the nightclub Arena Classic. But LGBTQ+ life (night or day) is not confined to the Eixample, and other landmarks include the BeGay *chiringuito* at Mar Bella, the LGBTQ+ nudist beach, as well as countless themed events held in the city during the summer. Barcelona's Pride is one of the biggest in Europe (although this is one instance where Barcelona loses out to Madrid), in June there is Fire, the international gay and lesbian film festival, and in August comes Circuit, a non-stop eleven-day festival with parties, DJs and music, divided between Mar Bella beach and the water park Illa Fantasia.

collective – like certain marine species that live in uninhabitable places. And yet there already was a native species living there who, it seems, nobody had noticed or bothered to consult: the residents of Barceloneta. I suppose that is why this neighbourhood has a long tradition of residents' protests, the history of which is beyond the scope of this article. A species in the throes of extinction, evidencing local activities, the so-called 'brown grand-fathers' (brown, as in dark skinned from the sun) playing dominoes.

I park my skates for a moment and commit to the investigation. An architect colleague of mine at the university, Dr Joan Maroto, advises me that the model for the port is included in the urban plan (or 'Barcelona model'), a mixture of architec-ture and urban planning created by Oriol Bohigas, which was widely implemented at the time of the Olympics (something that has been well discussed in a book by Llàtzer Moix, *La Ciudad de los Arquitectos* ['The Architects' City']). This method of creating a city was wholly reliant on design and on designers (to the exclusion of the resi-dents) as transforming agents of the urban reality, social, political and economic.

I have an impertinent question. Why did nobody think about me? This beach doesn't represent me. I'm a citizen of Barcelona. I pay my taxes. I made my home here because I like to have the sea close by as a necessary limit to construction. I find peace in large expanses of water. When I arrived here from Girona, my birthplace, I fell in love with the golden light of September (which I have only ever seen in this port city) and with the city's open character, hungry for ideas and novelty. After years of ignoring each other, during the pandemic, for the first time ever, the beach smelled of the sea, and it was a peaceful place to take a night-time stroll, like the ones I enjoyed on the Costa Brava of my youth. It was then, as a positive contrast (normality being the counter-point), that I understood how mass tourism erodes and dilutes relationships. In recent years Barcelona's beach has been an extension of the airport, a place with little identity or deep connections, a *non*-place with which only a handful of locals courageously insisted on identi-fying. Despite all its terrible consequences, Covid had driven all that away for a time, and suddenly one could see familiar faces more often. Everything was less eroded, including the water. The nursing staff at the Hospital del Mar would bring some of the patients suffering from the new virus outside to look at the horizon and breathe in the breeze that would help them get well. That sea-breeze smell did not last long. With the lifting of lockdown the smell of fried food from the beach restau-rants once more clouded the horizon that I usually seek out on other stretches of the coastline.

I undertake a search of news reports relating to the most famous buildings and icons on the local coastal skyline – all of them, it goes without saying, projects by architects and artists of the male gender.

'The upmarket marina that the Hotel Arts had planned is in tatters,' according to one newspaper. 'This latter-day Titan of the coastline purchased its own access to the Barcelona beach for €76 million in October 2020. As part of the controversial transaction, the five-star Archer Hotel Capital was to open a shopping and dining zone connected directly to the Somorrostro bathing area.' This is the first headline. All this luxury has an ancient and very humble origin: the Somorrostro Beach. There are no records that explain the origin of the name or the date that the area began to

'But what would a feminist city be like? It would have more space for its residents, and it would put people's lives at the centre.'

be populated. One hypothesis is that the name came from the Somorrostro region in the Basque Country through a group of Basque fishermen who settled in the area in the mid-19th century. Towards the middle of the 20th century there were successive waves of immigration from the south of Spain, and Gypsies built shacks on the beach between the Hospital for Infectious Diseases (now the Hospital del Mar, located on the periphery of the Barceloneta district on the border with Poblenou) and the Lebon gasworks in Poblenou (now gone). The neighbourhood stretched all the way to the river Bogatell. Living conditions were precarious, and the shacks were frequently flooded by the sea. It was also used as a rubbish dump. I search for comments provided by users of these beaches. The first to appear in Google refers to Barceloneta Beach: 'Fond childhood memories ... [but] Somorrostro was *soooo* scary.' Why? I do another search and find the answer. There is a reference to Somorrostro as early as 1882. Around 1950 eighteen thousand people lived in the slum settlement, occupying some 1,400 shacks. It disappeared in 1966, coinciding with a visit by Francisco Franco to Barcelona to attend some naval exercises. The residents were transferred to homes built by the Obra Sindical del Hogar (a state-sponsored social-housing organisation), most of them in the Sant Roc district of Badalona. There was a substantial Roma community living in the Somorrostro shanty town. The flamenco dancer Carmen Amaya was born there. The settlement was immortalised in the 1963

film *Los Tarantos* in which Carmen Amaya herself played a Gypsy woman. 'What was life like there? Bad, very bad. There was a lot of poverty. The worst years of my life, without a doubt.'

As the feminist geographer Jane Darke states in 'The Man-Shaped City' (in Chris Booth, Jane Darke and Susan Yeandle's *Changing Places: Women's Lives in the City*, Sage, 1996): 'Any settlement is an inscription in space of the social relations in the society that built it ... Our cities are patriarchy written in stone, brick, glass and concrete.'

But what would a feminist city be like? It would have more space for its residents, and it would put people's lives at the centre; we already know that and have an example – I am referring here to the first, praiseworthy attempt at reparation in the superblocks of Poblenou, which prioritise pedestrians over motor vehicles (see 'Superblock 503' on page 57). It would also have more security measures for women and vulnerable groups travelling at night.

But what about symbols and icons? Could we feminise the vertical architectural metaphor? Why has that not occurred to anyone yet? Skateless, I carry on skating in my thoughts. Would it be possible to insert into this skyline of phallic profiles the roundness of a breast, à la Bandini? Could the local skyline be a little less penetrative and a little more nutritive? We have a hotel in the shape of a sail, Mariscal's giant prawn in the Port Vell and Frank Gehry's giant fish. If we're going to have an iconic review of the symbolic order to which our maritime

A young woman taking part in Marcela Hattemer's Rolling Retro Barcelona skating classes, which have brought old-school quad skates back into fashion.

architecture alludes, it is worthwhile noting the large amount of Western feminine mythology associated with water and fluidity. In the West these symbols have a menacing connotation. Take, for example, the sirens, an archetype that has evolved under the gaze of those who contemplate it from the Greek tradition down to the Romantics, both sharing its fatalist condition. According to one study: 'There is no doubt that the attribution of deceit to the sirens is derived from the Greek concept, *métis* (cunning), which is more applicable to their antagonist, Ulysses, who in the classical tradition is the "*polymétis*", someone "fertile in resources".' In fact, the notion that the naiads or other aquatic women attract men to their 'enchanted places' where the latter disappear, can be seen in the myth of Hylas, a friend of Hercules, who vanishes when he goes to fetch some water from a spring. His supposed abduction by nymphs explains his disappearance, although in this case it is not portrayed as the result of any deceit. In the same way the conflation of the siren with the image of a lecherous woman is nothing more than another moralistic rereading of the classical siren, and clearly the serpent woman of folklore dazzles not so much by her powers of seduction as by her magical, thaumaturgic qualities. For example, it is Melusine who is fleeing from her husband, not the other way around, and the same thing occurs in similar legends. In a more modern setting, Hans Christian Andersen's sirens, like the Little Mermaid, remind us of those who were struck dumb for falling in love with a man.

My architectonic imagination cannot avoid diving in and exploring the panoply of aquatic symbols: pavilions like bivalve molluscs, sirens and medusas mixing in between Gehry's fish and Mariscal's prawn. They will be the new icons of the coastline. Let us remember that when Medusa was raped by the Lord of the Sea, Poseidon, in Athena's own temple, the enraged goddess turned the girl's beautiful hair into a bed of snakes. Medusa, I suspect, could occupy a spot on the seafront in homage to all women who have been sexually assaulted in these parts – there must be more than a few, especially in the nightlife entertainment zone, if the newspapers are right – and as a symbol of protection. I travel to the past and discover new meanings: let's start with something like this (from *The Odyssey*: Book XIII):

At the head of this harbour there is a large olive tree, and nearby a pleasant, shaded grotto sacred to the nymphs known as naiads. Within the cave there are mixing jars and stone amphorae, and bees also make their honey there. Inside, there are also great stone looms on which the nymphs weave a cloth with a purple dye – a wonder to behold! – and there are constantly flowing waters. There are two entrances, one facing north through which mortals can enter, the other to the south which is for the gods, and men cannot enter through here: it is a route for immortals only.

And now I can picture the naiads in their bathing costumes, roller-skaters, surfers paddle-surfing across the waves, their friends keeping an eye on the children, liberated inhabitants, beautiful and fearless. What an aspiration for my stretch of the sea. ✒

MIQUI OTERO
Translated by Kit Maude

GET OUT THERE ...

A sentimental journey through the history
and spirit of Barça, the football club
that has always been 'more than a club',
'the unarmed army of Catalonia'.

... AND ENJOY YOURSELVES

A football fan in Plaça de Catalunya, in front of the giant screen set up for the final of the 2022 Women's Champions League.

The idea that the best way to deal with bad news is to prepare for worse news is something that has been drummed in to Barça fans since the beginning – at least, it's always been that way for me.

My first *Blaugrana* idol didn't yet exist (outside of a comic book), and my very first memory as a *Culer* is of bawling my eyes out as I tried desperately to scratch a sticker that read 'Barça, Champions of Europe 1985–1986' off a Formica desk. (We'd lost.) I was five years old and had pretty much taught myself to read from Eric Castel comics, which featured a French character with salt-and-pepper hair and a powerful left foot inspired by the Italian forward Roberto Bettega. During Castel's golden age, which began in 1979, he came from Internazionale to win the hearts of Barça fans who, in the real world, had just lost Johan Cruyff, their most iconic player, 'a talent seemingly as fragile as a former drummer in the Beatles but with the cunning of a stockbroker', as Barcelona's most insightful critic, Manuel Vázquez Montalbán, once memorably described the Dutchman.

Cruyff had understood Barça's role as a political symbol very well, so much so that he gave his son the very Catalan name of Jordi, a gesture that earned him more acclaim even than the 5-0 thrashing of Real Madrid at the Bernabéu Stadium that happened while he was in charge. Years after he left, following Diego Maradona's unsuccessful tenure with the club, which I don't remember at all, I would console myself with another fictional hero far greater and more photogenic than a Barça side that had never won the European Cup. Perhaps I'm still looking for that kind of escape from the mediocrity of life. Perhaps that's why I write novels rather than, say, becoming a youth-team coach.

On that 7 May 1986 I was climbing the stairs to my classroom at primary school when a classmate grabbed my comic, tearing a page that showed Castel scoring a goal in the top corner. I didn't mind; I didn't even see it as a bad omen. We were all overexcited because that night Barça would win the European Cup. They weren't just *playing* in the final, they were going to *win*. Their opponents were an unfancied team from Romania (Steaua Bucharest) and not only that but the match would be held in Seville, meaning the stadium would be a sea of blue and burgundy. We were so sure that we would be lifting the cup that night (in fact, the grown-ups had been raising plenty of cups in bars for hours already) that, the day before, a sports newspaper had begun distributing stickers with the word 'Champions' surrounded by a cloud of blue-and-burgundy confetti. As Franco said about his regime in 1969, 'it's all wrapped up tight'. So, in class, I taped the comic back together and then stuck the triumphant sticker – which (I remember well) was almost twice the size of my hand – on to the desk.

The city was in euphoric mood with not a thought given to that other final defeat, an accursed game against Benfica played in Berne on 31 May 1961. I could be forgiven for that, given that it happened twenty years before I was born – but the makers of the presumptuous stickers could not. That night Barça had lost after hitting the

MIQUI OTERO is a journalist and writer who started out working for record labels and festivals. He writes for *El País* and *El Periódico* and works for the radio stations RAC1 and Onda Cero as well as teaching literature and journalism at the University of Barcelona. He has published four novels; the latest, *Simón* (Blackie Books, 2020), has been translated into a number of languages.

The name given to Barça fans, *Culers* (or *Culés* in Spanish), dates back to the 1910s when the team played at the Camp de la Indústria. The small ground had a capacity of only six thousand, which was insufficient for the number of fervent fans, so they started to use the stadium wall as an extra back row of seats. This meant that from the street the only thing passers-by could see was a series of backsides perched on the wall, hence the nickname (from *cul*, meaning bottom), which was also adopted by a famous 1990s cartoon character representing the quintessential Barça fan, Jordi Culé.

post, which in those days were square, four times. Their bad luck was such that immediately after the match the international footballing authorities declared that goalposts would be rounded from then on, said change coming a little too late for us.

I don't remember much about the next final. No one seemed to want to score that night. I know that it went to penalties and, most importantly, that we lost. I know that I was sleepy and that I cried. And I know that the next day the teacher ordered me to remove the hubristic sticker from my desk, a task that took me days because I'd bitten my nails to the quick on the fateful night. Then there was the mockery from my fellow pupils; the comic book-tearing menace's cackle was especially cutting.

I'd always been a Barça fan, but I grew even more committed following that ordeal, which gave me an education in what it really meant to be a supporter as well as the dangers of overconfidence, vanity – and biting your nails.

The fact that in the fictional world Castel would eventually sign for Paris Saint-Germain was also excellent preparation for a similar transfer, Messi's move to the same club when I was an adult, but back then it didn't matter nearly so much as events in the real world where, shortly after that cup-final defeat, Cruyff would return to Camp Nou as manager, having swapped his beatnik hairdo for a detective's trench coat. And it was he who relieved us of our congenital pessimism and childhood trauma with the advice he'd give in the changing room before the next big European final, our third, in 1992, a phrase that I try to apply to my life and work and which I repeat to my son, who's now about the age I was when I was hopelessly scratching away at that sticker, a motto that Barça has always sought to live up to, pursuing it like a mythical beast: 'Get out there and enjoy yourselves.'

*

A Barcelona fan in a bar near Camp Nou before a league game.

In August 2021 Lionel Messi confirmed that he was leaving. After the departure of the best player in the club's history, this was Barça: a child-sized figurine in a shop window on the Ramblas wearing the team's second kit from a couple of years ago and an oversized cap that had slipped down around its eyes. A pitiful sight. On its chest was a sign that read 'Sale: 50% off'.

The mannequin is still there in what is a typical souvenir shop full of football paraphernalia, T-shirts with supposedly amusing slogans and mariachi hats bought by tourists apparently in the mistaken belief that Barcelona is in Mexico. It's not the only crumbling hangover from a glorious recent past or the only indicator of the present decline, but it was well suited to the atmosphere during the pandemic. In other shops on the avenue, which runs from the city centre to the sea, one can see dolls of players who left the club some time ago, like Neymar Jr or Luis Suárez. Some dangle by a thread from the ceiling, making it look as though they've been hanged, like mementos from a lost battle.

When Joan Laporta, one of the architects of the glorious Pep Guardiola era of 2008–12, returned as club president in 2021, he denounced the previous board of directors. He informed the authorities of irregularities and a debt of €1.35 billion. In just three years the previous president, Josep Maria Bartomeu, had increased the wage bill by 61 per cent and overseen a succession of unsuccessful signings. In fact, the calamitous descent began with the signing of Neymar Jr, which was shrouded in suspicion and subject to several investigations, accompanied by the notorious fax sent by Messi in which he threatened to leave. Or perhaps it was the day the Spanish state forcibly, and illegally, suppressed attempts to implement the

TROUBLED TIMES

It was a Sunday afternoon, and Sandro Rosell, ex-president of FC Barcelona and the architect of major transfers like the purchase of Neymar Jr, was listening to his beloved club's game on the radio. This was not a form of nostalgia for football before the pay-TV era; Rosell was in a prison cell where he would spend two years in connection with allegations of money laundering and criminal conspiracy (for which he was later acquitted) as well facing accusations of corruption, fraud and tax evasion around Neymar's transfer to Barça. Officially, the Brazilian star's 2013 move cost €57 million, but the club later admitted that the real sum paid out was €86 million. Rosell was replaced by his deputy Josep Maria Bartomeu (a member of the Catalan club since joining in 1974 at the age of eleven), who was in office from 2014 to 2020, and, in his turn, engulfed by the so-called 'Barçagate' scandal. Two *Cadena Ser* journalists discovered that the president had appointed the firm I3 Ventures to discredit a number of players he had taken against, including Messi and Piqué, using fake social media profiles. The million euros spent on mudslinging had been divided up into instalments of €200,000 each (as to pass contracts and invoices above that figure would have required the approval of the members' assembly) thus keeping them under the radar. In spite of the club's international reach, having fans all around the world, 90 per cent of its members live in Catalonia and 60 per cent in the metropolitan area of Barcelona. In total, there are 150,000 members, who elect the president following no-holds-barred election campaigns. Bartomeu was replaced at the top by Joan Laporta, who had been president between 2003 and 2010, a fervent supporter of Catalan independence and another figure who has had to face a number of scandals.

results of the referendum on Catalonian independence and the board decided to allow the match scheduled at Camp Nou that afternoon to be played behind closed doors – and the results on the pitch didn't help much.

In just a few years Barça had gone broke after being one of the most financially powerful clubs in the world, but that wasn't the most important issue. Its image (presidents arrested and/or imprisoned, accusations of espionage and defamation of their own players, etc.) was terrible, and it no longer represented Catalan identity, something that had had such meaning during the dark years of the fascist regime.

Montalbán once described the club as 'Catalonia's unarmed army', meaning that Catalonia might be a nation without a state, but even so it had a national club. It was a means of integration for outsiders – my parents, for example, who migrated from Galicia to Barcelona the year Cruyff arrived. For a time, Barça presented itself as an institution more democratic than the Spanish dictatorship, and even today it sells itself as the only democracy among the planet's footballing elite. The justification for this claim lies in its 140,000 members, of whom more than 110,000 vote in club elections; 26.74 per cent are women, and 93 per cent, despite the club's global reach, live and work in Catalonia. Barça is an oligarchic democracy controlled by the Catalan bourgeoisie in which hereditary lineages abound. During periods of oppression, the wealthy classes invest money in the club to counteract the expansion of centrist imperialism, which they identify with Real Madrid. Although today income from membership fees only accounts for 6 per cent of the club's turnover (in the past that percentage has been as much as ten times higher), members still regard the

THERE IS ANOTHER TEAM …

Besides Barça and Espanyol, Barcelona also has a third football club with more than a century of history, which, despite having been stuck in the lower divisions for years, helped to write the history of sport in Catalonia and Spain. Named Europa (currently known officially as Club Esportiu Europa), it was established to represent the Gràcia district. The club boasts a white-and-blue kit with a distinctive V-shaped scapular design, a modern stadium, a great museum and a flourishing youth scheme that favours talent from the neighbourhood. It enjoyed a golden age in the 1920s, and by defeating Barça in the 1922–3 Copa Catalunya it won the right to enter the Spanish Championship (forerunner of the Copa del Rey rather than La Liga) and reached the final only to lose to Athletic Club Bilbao. The runner-up spot was enough for Europa to claim its seat among the leading clubs who founded La Liga in 1929, however, and to take part in the opening tournament of the Primera División. Europa lasted three seasons in the Primera before being relegated following the advent of professionalism and the consequent hike in costs, and the team has never yet made it back into the top flight. Europa also stands out as a multi-sports club – it was, for example, the first club to play an official basketball match in Spain; the year was 1922, and the opposition was Laietà, also from Barcelona. In recent years the club has taken a position in favour of the use of the Catalan language and the freeing of the jailed separatist leaders – although it has not openly supported 'yes' to secession, it has defended the right to decide on the issue via referendum. In 2001 it amended its statutes, declaring itself in black and white to be a sporting club that is 'antifascist and opposed to male chauvinism, homophobia, racism and bullying'.

An Eric Castel comic at the Sunday second-hand books market in Sant Antoni.

club as something that belongs to them – and not just symbolically. They have plenty of reasons to think so.

Of the 200,000 Spanish citizens murdered by the fascist dictator Francisco Franco, one of the first, on 6 August 1936, was Josep Sunyol, the president of Barça. After they took the city, the victors tried to use the stadium as a place to park their tanks. The *Culer* team even went on a tour of Latin America to drum up support for the Republican cause. Franco's involvement in the Argentinian star Alfredo Di Stéfano's signing with Real Madrid over Barcelona in the early 1950s has always been suspected: originally it had looked as though he was headed to Barça but ended up becoming a key figure during one of their arch-rival's most successful eras.

Of course, back then nothing was black or white, but, as the writer Francisco Casavella put it, 'it was all in black and white' (in this case mostly white). The Catalan bourgeoisie sought to adapt to the new regime, although Barça, where it was forbidden to speak Catalan or use the language on banners, was always, albeit quietly, a pragmatic force for resistance to the Franco regime. If you couldn't speak your language out loud you'd do your talking on the pitch.

In 1968 club president Narcís de Carreras ran an election campaign with the slogan 'Barcelona is something more than a football club'. This would later be shortened to 'More than a club', a tagline with which Barça has promoted itself ever since. That 'more' includes the consolation of a losing side who, aware that they can't win, cherish other values. It has evolved over time and is now associated with anti-Franco symbolism, the beautiful modern style of the Cruyffist game, its branches in other sports, the intention not to advertise on the team shirt and then doing so with the UNICEF logo and an operating philosophy very much in the style of Catalan industry: global but local, control reserved to a few families but nonetheless managing to capture the hearts (and wallets) of a whole people. 'More than a club' is a vaccine against the internal contradictions of a massive club adapting to the dynamics of modern football, including commercial agreements with countries with murky records.

One of Barcelona's world-famous attractions was an albino gorilla. Catalonia has a black virgin. The biggest star Barça has ever had barely speaks. For years the city presented itself as modern and different because it knew it couldn't compete with centrist public policy and the financial clout of the national capital. All that is Barça, too. It's a family that experiences conflicts but is also resilient, one that strives to make history repeat itself in order to preserve its identity. Which is why today, although the club hasn't matched the glory of previous decades, even though it is losing, Barça is beginning to believe again. (Maybe someone will finally remove that figurine from the shop on the Ramblas.) The reason for this, in addition to a new batch of excellent 'homemade' players, brought up with 'Barça DNA', is the new manager, Xavi Hernández. During his playing years he didn't score many goals or rack up many assists, but he was still a club legend. 'She can't sing or dance, but you won't want to miss her,' so ran an American advertisement promoting the arrival in the US of Spanish actress and singer Lola Flores. Xavi might not have been able to do everything, but he knew how to play the Barça way like nobody else – and now he's sitting in the manager's chair.

Xavi returned as an emergency appointment midway through the season, promising to restore the style of Cruyff and Guardiola. Flaubert said that 'style is an absolute way of seeing the world', and the sentiment applies to how many *Culers* see their club.

Barça has always had close connections to the Catholic Church, but it has another Holy Trinity worshipped almost as fervently as the Christian one: the Father is Cruyff, Guardiola is the Son, and the Holy Spirit (or son of the son) is Xavi. They represent total football. A Barcelona fan will be happy enough if, regardless of results and a poor present situation, they have a style and a promising future. Used to losing, as I learned during the sticker episode, they're in love with the idea of being Barça in spite of everything.

*

And yet the team that had grown accustomed to losing started to win. And they won with a new kind of football. 'Playing football is very simple, but playing simple football is the hardest thing in the world,' said the first Messiah.

We're back with the second coming of Cruyff, the climax of whose tenure came at the European Cup Final in London at Wembley against Sampdoria in 1992. Only someone who wore Ray-Ban aviators and a Philip Marlowe trench coat with a self-confident genius that bordered on delusion could bring an end to the fatalism that came with square posts and stickers on a desk. Cruyff had amazed the world as a footballer, but he was also the manager who best understood the game. He was, in sports writer Simon Kuper's words, 'both Edison and the lightbulb'.

That spring of 1992 the city was dressed to impress, drunk on an almost childish excitement and a sense of belonging that was perfectly suited to an eleven-year-old like me. That summer the Olympic Games would be held in Barcelona, and Barça had

THE PASSENGER   Miqui Otero

the chance to win their first European Cup. Barça was still quite different from what it is today: for example, the shirt didn't have any advertising and it was made by Meyba, a Catalan firm that started out selling flip-flops and swimming costumes in the beach neighbourhood of Barceloneta.

When he saw that his players were racked with nerves, Cruyff opted against grand speechifying and just said the magic words 'Get out there and enjoy yourselves', words that are now engraved on the pedestal of the statue of Cruyff that was erected at Camp Nou some years later.

The game ended with a nil-nil score-line that threatened to revive old fears. All the signs seemed to point to it being decided on penalties, just as before. But now Cruyff was there. Foul in the 112th minute. Stoichkov taps it, Bakero stops it and Koeman scores an amazing goal. Then he goes to ask the referee the time. Even today, when I've had one beer too many, you'll hear me bellowing the following words in the street, 'Schmidhuber, there's still a minute to go!'

Cruyff was special, and he showed it with both his play and his good luck during that period. He arrived for the first time as a player in the 1970s, when Spain was still stuck in the 1950s. He came from Ajax, where he'd trained since he still had his baby teeth (he lived in a very poor neigh-bourhood a few metres from the stadium). He played cricket and baseball at the club, which was run along similar multi-sporting lines as Barça. He always said that his son was the first Jordi (the patron saint of Catalonia) after many years during which the dictatorship only allowed children to be baptised with the Castilian rendering of the name, Jorge. And then there was that modernity, hints of which appeared when he arrived and would be presented to the world during the Barcelona Olympic

EL CLÁSICO

When an El Clásico match (between FC Barcelona and Real Madrid) is played, history, politics, economics and identity become entangled in a climate of reciprocal suspicion and controversy. The first issues date back to 1916, when Barça left the field in protest against the refereeing, a move they wanted to repeat in 1943, although legend has it that officials from the Franco regime sent the Catalans back on to the pitch at gunpoint. The major event of the 1950s was the soap opera surrounding the Argentinian Alfredo Di Stéfano's move to Real: both Barça and Real had signed agreements for his transfer and, to resolve this, the Spanish Football Federation decided that the striker would have to alternate, playing for two years in Madrid and two in Barcelona, but ultimately Real won the tug of war. Helenio Herrera, coach at Barça from 1958 to 1960, admitted to having motivated those players with Catalan roots by leveraging their pro-independence sentiments, a leitmotif of the Clásico fixture that became further inflamed in the 2010s when banners appeared at Camp Nou emblazoned with the slogan 'Catalonia is not Spain'. In 2019 the match was even postponed for public-order reasons. Defecting to the rival club provokes genuine outrage, as Luís Figo discovered when returning to Barcelona in a Real kit to be greeted with pigs' heads, knives and billiard balls. Despite the hatred – Günter Netzer, midfielder for Real from 1973 to 1976, recalled that every foreigner who arrived in the dressing room was immediately informed that the club's bitter enemy hailed from Catalonia – the Spanish crowds still know how to appreciate class: when being substituted, both Ronaldinho and Iniesta have been applauded by opposition fans.

A boy playing football after school in Poblenou.

'In the *Blaugrana* stands, a less tangible quality is valued greater still: charm.'

Games. It was something that could be sensed on the pitch.

His footballing aphorisms, uttered in impenetrable, gnomic Spanish, are little works of art. Involuntary haikus. They draw on the idea of total football (all the footballers dancing together, interchanging positions, creating triangular overloads, attack as the best defence) which he had first experienced at Ajax as a player. My forward is my first defender and my goalkeeper my last attacker. If you have the ball, they can't score a goal. It's about making the pitch small when you don't have the ball and big when you do. People talk about legs, but football is played with the brain, being in the right place at the right time. Play as though you could never make a mistake, but don't be surprised when you do. And get out there and enjoy yourselves.

*

Cruyff, who was a guiding spirit for the club and its philosophy while he was alive and has remained so since his death, once said that Messi was the most spectacular player, but that Xavi was the best.

It is said that when he arrived as manager he removed a sign on the wall establishing a minimum height for entrance into the Barça youth academies. I'm not surprised that Barça is popular with children: they see themselves reflected in the club. Messi is only 1.64 metres tall, Andrés Iniesta 1.71, Xavi 1.7, and of the new crop of home-grown players who are now starring in the first team, the general favourite (more popular even than Ansu Fati and his magical goal-scoring touch) is a weedy-looking kid who

weighs a mere sixty kilos and measures 1.74 metres in height, Pedri.

And so we return to the present day. Pedri has all the qualities known to seduce Barcelona fans. He's quietly spoken off the pitch but eloquent with the ball at his feet. He knows what he's going to do a couple of seconds before the other twenty-one players do. His apparent shyness contrasts with his self-confidence. He doesn't go in for tattoos and crazy hairstyles – he'd be a mother-in-law's delight. He's a short midfielder. His elegance is more economical than showy. He has such mastery of the ball that he might as well take it home with him at the end of the day and bring it back the next. Even though he was already a teenager when he arrived at the club, his grandfather had founded the *Blaugrana* bar on Tenerife, and ever since he was little he'd eaten his meals on crockery adorned with the club crest. At Barça the directors come from distinguished families with long associations with the club, membership cards are either inherited or given as a christening present, the biggest stars (Guardiola, for instance) worked as busboys at the stadium and the players share footballing genes.

Xavi is already comparing Pedri with Iniesta, although his statistics are actually better than those of the Manchego wizard at the same age. In his first season, when he was only just old enough to get a driving license and vote, he touched the ball an average of fifty-eight times per game; the next that rose to sixty-six. In one famous match against Juventus, the precocious teenager touched the ball sixty-four times and made forty-one passes with a 95 per cent success rate. It's funny how numbers matter in the beautiful game, in a similar way to proportions in art. But, even so, in the *Blaugrana* stands, a less tangible quality is valued greater still: charm.

Barça has repeatedly experienced defeats, and non-sporting-related scandals, too. Sometimes it's worrying in Camp Nou to see members selling their seats to tourists; it threatens to dilute the atmosphere in the stadium (which is usually quiet and tense) and the club personality. But with Pedri in the team, Cruyff's great-grandson, Guardiola's grandson, the son of Xavi, Iniesta and Messi, the fans can trust in a line from *The Count of Monte Cristo*: 'Be patient, and have faith.'

*

I have had the following nightmare on more than one occasion. A minute before the starting whistle at a Real Madrid–Barça match, the teams swap shirts. The players who a few seconds earlier you'd hated are wearing the blue and burgundy, and your idols are now decked out in white. Who do you cheer for? What do you do? Apart from mopping the sweat from your brow, that is. The nightmare always ends with the whistle, which wakes me up and returns me to a world of certainties. There is no homeland more important than childhood, and we are never more faithful to it than in the colours of the team we supported as a child. Even when we lose.

Or win. A feeling of unreality haunted me often during the first decade and a half of the 21st century when Barça was under the reign (in terms of play, titles and aesthetics) of Messi and Guardiola.

Sergi Pàmies, a Barça fan and writer who grew up in France (his parents fled the Franco regime), wrote a book about being a bad *Culer* because living abroad meant he found it hard to hate the enemy as much as he should. And for a boy schooled in the

difficult art of finding victory in defeat it was very hard to assimilate the fact that for a time we were imperious, the way the bad guys had always been.

Since his debut in a friendly in 2003 Messi represented the promise of a new era. And his back story worked perfectly. His first contract was signed on the back of a napkin, a commitment to pay for treatment for a growth disorder. We'd watched the kid grow into an atomic flea from a very young age. He was an almost pathologically shy leader; he didn't have the charisma of a Kubala or Cruyff. During celebrations of a domestic league title, shortly before winning another Champions League, he said, 'I'll give a speech when we've brought it home.' During the celebrations for said title, he was passed the microphone, and the crowd prepared itself to savour every word. 'The truth is, I have nothing to say,' he said to a packed stadium. 'He only talks on the pitch,' I remarked to a friend in the bar where we were celebrating.

We loved Messi in spite of his reticence. We watched both his football and eloquence improve year on year. We suffered whenever we saw him sadly trudging across the pitch, his eyes on the ground as though he were looking for a lost penny. We have celebrated his slaloms. To understand his magic, I recommend Jordi Puntí's *Todo Messi: Ejercicios de Estilo* ('All About Messi: Exercises in Style'), in which he says that Messi realises Italo Calvino's predictions for the new millennium: 'lightness, speed, precision, vision and multiplicity'.

He transcends football. That genius of mime Jacques Tati called Cruyff the player an artist, and Nureyev said that he was a dancer. Messi has been compared with Mozart and Picasso. Messi made us happy, which is why his departure from the club left us as bereft as adults without a job and as sad as kids without a ball. We won four of our five Champions League titles when he was in the team. With him, we beat Madrid. We thrashed them. And that in itself seemed strange. Having him in the team was an automatic advantage, like we had the magic potion that helped Asterix and his village to hold back the Romans.

The duels with Madrid throughout that period were epic. Especially the ones in the 2010–11 season. Madrid, at a loss for the first time ever, felt powerless. José Mourinho, their manager, tried to undermine Messi's talent with the dark arts of a Marvel villain: he even poked one of Pep Guardiola's assistants in the eye. The Madrid-supporting media sneered that Pep 'pissed cologne'. We were better on the pitch, but, more than that, the fans enjoyed their moral superiority, or at least the semblance of it. We boasted about our humility, took pride in our modesty. All that has gone to hell in recent years. Those duels between Madrid's insecure arrogance and Barça's passive-aggressive cunning prefigured, many said, the dynamic of the 'Procés' years when Catalan institutions flirted with challenging the Spanish state, which did not hesitate to suppress them.

All that remains of that now is nostalgia for the past, a promising future and shirts with his name on the back on the Ramblas. Perhaps tourists think we still want to believe, that we can't accept that Messi has gone. After all, Eric Castel came back from Paris Saint-Germain.

*

The 21st century is the women's century, and in Barcelona plenty of girls wear official shirts with a name on the back that isn't Pedri, Gavi, Ansu Fati or Messi but rather Alexia – although shirts featuring new signing Robert Lewandowski sold out quickly at the beginning of the 2022–3 season.

If Barça sees itself as more than a club, Alexia Putellas is much more than a football player. She's an example to all those girls who might once have been relegated to watching in the playground but now want to score goals themselves. She sells more shirts than Pedri, has appeared on more *monas* (the chocolate cake given to Catalan children at Easter) than Messi last year, and *caganers* (the quirky folk figures in our Christmas nativity scenes) featuring her image sell out. On the feast day of the patron saint of Catalonia, Sant Jordi, in 2022 – a day when books are a traditional gift – more volumes were released about the women's first team than the men's.

It's not always easy to determine the moment when everything changes. Here it is. On 30 March 2022 Camp Nou recorded its largest ever attendance for a women's football match: 91,553 fans watched the second leg of the Champions League quarter final against Real Madrid. Until relatively recently it would have been unheard of for them to play in the main stadium. Today they're filling it and breaking records.

It's not just that Alexia is the current holder of the footballer of the year Ballon d'Or or that Barça's women are winning while the men are losing, it is also the symbolic weight of players whose work extends beyond scoring goals to involvement in foundations for the rights of African sportswomen, raising awareness of LGBTQ+ issues and other political stances. Today elite sportswomen are saying things that sportsmen (because of their commercial commitments, apathy or simply because they're so out of touch with the real world) do not.

The story began a long time ago but

Mural of Alexia Putellas, star of the Barcelona women's team, in Plaça d'En Joanic.

'Today elite sportswomen are saying things that sportsmen (because of their commercial commitments, apathy or simply because they're so out of touch with the real world) do not.'

was only consolidated quite recently. In 1970, while Franco was still alive, a brave eighteen-year-old called Inmaculada Cabecerán managed to arrange a meeting with the Barça president. During their thirty-minute encounter she explained why they should have a women's team. The club expressed interest without offering much practical support, so she had to do the same thing as Joan Gamper had when, in 1899, he placed an ad in the newspaper inviting people to come and play for the team he'd just founded. For the women, the advertisement appeared in the pages of the *Revista Barcelonista* fan magazine, inviting players between the ages of eighteen and twenty-five to get involved. And so the adventure began, although the team wouldn't become official until 2002.

With the current players Barça is clearly winning 'something more than cups'. Where Cruyff said that his brilliant, imaginative style of total football was the product of the countercultural liberation of the 1960s, professionalisation and mass support for women's football (which is beautiful, impressive, evolving and charismatic) came following the #MeToo movement in a century that will surely be both female and feminist.

The success of the women's team also reinforces the idea of a club that is bigger than the men's football team. The concept

was there right from the club's foundation as a multi-sport institution. Barça has professional teams in basketball, handball and inline hockey that have given it just as many – or more – glorious afternoons as the men's football team. But it also runs professional and amateur teams in almost every sport you can imagine: athletics, rugby, volleyball, ice hockey, figure skating, wheelchair basketball, swimming, cycling, baseball and even Greco-Roman wrestling. Even though some of these activities lose money, each enhances Barça's character. It's no great leap to see a synergy between the different branches: Cruyff would wait to have breakfast with the handball manager, while Guardiola took on assistants from the water polo team.

The day that Barça gives up on them, surrendering to the business logic of modern football, it will cease to be Barça – or at least it will cease to be more than a club. Of course, that's not something the kid who had to scratch the champions sticker off the desk after the lost final would stand for, the same kid who now brings this text – which, for him, has been 'something more than an article' – to a close with some words of advice to visitors to the city, a phrase that won't be sullied by immoral financial jackals or hulking central defenders: 'Get out there and enjoy yourselves.' 🏴

'Offices to Let'

Does it make sense to create a high-tech district boasting innovative projects if its streets empty out in the evenings? Anna Pacheco takes us to the city's 22@ district, a former industrial area in the Poblenou neighbourhood, which achieves the feat of being both extremely lively and otherworldly.

ANNA PACHECO
Translated by Kathryn Phillips-Miles

Barcelona at dawn seen from the Carretera de les Aigües in Collserola Park.

'Distrct 22@ kills me. The buildings are more and more disturbing. There is a touch of irony about all this. As you walk along you know you want to be impressed. For example, that building on Carrer de Tànger, you can hear the sounds of a nursery coming from around the first floor where adults look after children during the working day. When you walk past the building you can't be entirely sure who's crying because the façade rises up like a wall and it's covered in tropical plants. I always think the people who are crying are the adults caked in poo with their clocking-in cards hanging around their necks. I picture them crawling around, and some of them have a business-like resilience, but they never give orders standing up, so the whole thing is a little grotesque. Of course they're crying, and of course they're calling for their mothers. No one wants to be there.'

A few months ago I published this piece on social media; it's a rather dystopian vision of employment in the city of Barcelona's technology district, where I have pounded the streets relentlessly over the last ten years. My life fits into a tiny map, just as the sociologist Paul-Henry Chombart illustrated in his *Trajets Pendant un An d'une Jeune Fille du XVIe Arrondissement*, published in 1957. For the girl from Paris (the subject of Chombart's study) the vertices are her home, the university and her piano teacher's home. My vertices criss-cross each other on a small number of streets, a small number of bars and a small number of banks. I went to a state university here, and I've worked here, too. We constantly move around the same areas, and I sometimes feel that the 22@ district is one big office that I will always return to, at least for as long as I have work.

A few people who work there reacted to the publication of my piece with comments such as 'oppressive' or 'how funny'. Someone recognised the nursery building from some of the photos I attached and told me with a sad-face emoji that they had the misfortune to work there. One woman told me that there was a gym on the third floor in the building opposite, and that at night, when it's dark, you can see men running on treadmills, and it looks at times as if they're trying to escape from something. My sister told me that it was her favourite place and that she'd always wanted to work there, and another woman told me that she loved her office, and yet another woman asked, half offended, 'What's so bad about 22@? I don't get it.'

I find this disparity really invigorating, and it is an example of the friction that exists within this space, a place that is both in the vanguard and in decline, a place that is reaching outwards in multiple directions and that perhaps once aspired to being something quite different from what it has become. This urban plan, centred on the Poblenou neighbourhood, was approved in 2000 and has been disrupted by successive financial crises. The first superblock in the city – a

ANNA PACHECO (Barcelona, 1991) is a narrative journalist and a writer who focuses on social and work issues, feminism and popular culture with a class perspective. Her work has appeared in journals such as *VICE*, *El País*, *Playground*, *El Salto* and *La Marea*. She is currently working as a freelance journalist and contributes to radio and TV programmes on Radio Primavera Sound and TV3. She has been published in a number of anthologies and is the author of *Listas, Guapas, Limpias* (Caballo de Troya, 2019), her first novel.

'There is something wild and exuberant about the skyscrapers here, something that forces you to look at them.'

scheme unique to Barcelona that aims to pacify and pedestrianise streets and that has attracted international interest (see 'Superblock 503' on page 57) – is also located in this neighbourhood. On a single street in 22@ it is quite usual to come across large co-working spaces with wooden pallets placed alongside broad-leaved plants, workers from technology companies drinking €3.50 café lattes, enormous posters advertising 'offices to let' and men (mostly from sub-Saharan Africa) pushing supermarket trolleys on the hunt for scrap metal.

If a person looked down on all this from above and wondered what it was all about, they would immediately notice that one of the city's iconic constructions, the Agbar Tower, is located in this neighbourhood. The building is shaped like a bullet, a suppository or, in the words of its architect Jean Nouvel, it is 'like a geyser rising from the depths of the sea'. There is something wild and exuberant about the skyscrapers here, something that forces you to look at them. Architecturally, this neighbourhood is an anomaly within the city. There are no narrow streets nor any of the modernist buildings for which the city is famous. The newbuilds (housing technology companies but also publishing houses, media and festival companies) coexist with the remains of an industrial legacy that is still just about discernible. The offices of the audiovisual group Mediapro are located in 22@, as are those of Primavera Sound; one of Amazon's main centres is here along with Glovo, RBA, the headquarters of Facebook's 'Competence Call Center',

eDreams ODIGEO, King (the videogame multinational responsible for successes such as Candy Crush) and many others, not to mention universities and television companies. There is the constant sound of JCBs. There is always something under construction, and it is possible that that *something* is more office buildings.

One afternoon while on a break I met up with the urban anthropologist José Mansilla at the superblock that encompasses the four streets of Badajoz, Pallars, Llacuna and Tànger. He lives in the neighbourhood and has been studying its development over the past few years. He explained that, as in other neighbourhoods such as the Gothic Quarter, there is a moratorium on hotels, meaning that no more hotels can be built. If a hotel closes it cannot be replaced with another. The great achievement would be, he said, if the same thing happened with office buildings. Mansilla was part of the Repensem el 22@ (Rethink 22@) initiative, a neighbourhood movement that attempted to bring forward proposals for rethinking this urban-planning macro-project. In the report, which has now ground to a halt, the authors argue, among other measures, in favour of restricting the construction of additional office space. It is ironic that today there are more offices than workers working in them.

Other Poblenou residents all tell me the same thing: after six in the evening the streets in the financial district empty out because no one lives there. Within a couple of hours the superblock where we are right now, surrounded by workers and mothers and fathers with their children (there's a

Clockwise from top left: A pedestrian walking in front of Jean Nouvel's Agbar Tower; a camper van near the former industrial site of Can Ricart; graffiti protesting against the demolition of Can Ricart; inside a record shop in Poblenou.

In 2004 IBM and the Spanish government signed an agreement to build Europe's most powerful computer, so innovative, despite its relatively modest size, that it would consume less energy than other similar machines. Its name is MareNostrum, in part a reference to its location in Barcelona – the city being on the shores of the Mediterranean (Mare Nostrum, Our Sea, to the Romans) – but also to its potential for connecting different parts of the world in the name of science, the aim of the project being to create a highly advanced research instrument. Since 2004 some updates have been required; the machine that is now based at the Universitat Politecnica de Catalunya is MareNostrum 4, having been upgraded in 2017 after two previous upgrades in 2006 and 2012–13. In 2022 it finds itself significantly lower down the global league tables compared with its top-ten position at the time it was installed. It now ranks seventy-fourth in the world for power but remains crucial for its scientific applications, above all in the development of models to predict scenarios in meteorology, physics and medicine, including a project to simulate the human body to test futuristic treatments and operations. However, while it may no longer be up there with the leaders for computing power, it can claim to be for beauty: in 2018 it won Datacenter Dynamics' Most Beautiful Data Center in the World award – chiefly because the university, which is situated a late-19th-century aristocratic residence, installed it in a glass case in the only sufficiently large space it had available: a deconsecrated church, complete with a nave, aisles and a rose window.

temporary school close by), will become a ghost square. It is an area where there are very few signs of life after a certain time of day – although there are a some, such as social encounters dictated by the day's schedule, maybe spending a breaktime with a work colleague or waiting for a few minutes for your children to come out of the school. Sometimes you might even catch sight of groups of tourists who have come to check out the superblock.

Mansilla wonders if this constitutes the opposite of a square. Perhaps a square is somewhere to be, not to wait around in or just to pass through. Squares are spaces for social encounters, where things happen or where we make things happen. Waiting is still productive. I wonder whether squares by definition should be unproductive. The school next to the superblock is temporary, constructed from prefabricated units, and in a few years from now it will be moved somewhere else. The anthropologist wonders whether when the children leave, the square will become a square with no children.

There is a café in this superblock that from Monday to Friday serves workers, most of them young people between twenty-five and thirty-five years of age, many of them from elsewhere in Europe. Most of them are white and fashionably dressed – and that other word that appears inseparable from the popular imagination in Barcelona: cosmopolitan. It's a word used by many residents up and down the boulevard. One woman, whom I'll speak to later, calls them 'cosmoidiots', then she giggles and apologises. The furniture in this café follows simple Scandinavian lines, and, in fact, each time I come here (sometimes I have something to eat or drink when I'm feeling flush) I remember a work colleague who laughingly told me one day that it might just as well be in

At one time, particularly around the port area, Barcelona was home to numerous factories, often designed by important architects in the most disparate styles, from neoclassical to modernist. Access to the sea was what allowed the city to industrialise; lacking raw materials locally, Barcelona relied on ships to bring them in. The first sector to develop was the textiles industry, which remained the driving force up to the inter-war period, when Barcelona's industry diversified, expanding into the chemical and metalworking sectors but also into publishing. Entrepreneurs had access to the city's plentiful, highly skilled labour force, which was bolstered by large numbers of immigrants arriving from the interior. But it was very difficult to control because of its sheer mass: unionised, internationalist and united in ever-larger mutual-support associations, the workers scared the industrialists. As a result the factory owners adopted a new strategy, in line with the demands of the contemporary Renaixença movement, which, in the second half of the 19th century, had brought about a literary re-evaluation of the language of Barcelona; the revival of a nationalist tradition on a cultural, artistic and architectural level, far removed from the siren calls of internationalism, was accompanied by the relocation of the factories to outside the city to separate the workers from their agitator colleagues and force them to live in industrial colonies. Finally, the push towards the tertiary sector fuelled by the Olympics in 1992 turned Barcelona once and for all into a city of tourism and services, and the beautiful old factory buildings were converted into cultural centres.

Sweden as in Barcelona. There is something nondescript about this district, and Mansilla says that it resembles neighbourhoods such as La Défense in Paris or the European Quarter in Brussels. I think about Chombart's map of Paris: we travel around the same places over and over again, and sometimes it doesn't even matter where we are because everything is identical. Then I think that this need to be special is also, in its way, horrifying.

District 22@ was initiated about ten years ago, and it embodies a kind of vision of the future from the past – that is, something from the past that had designs on being something great in the future. Marina, who is around thirty and works in a sound studio, says that's exactly why she loves it, that there is something here that never quite materialised. 'A frustrated Silicon Valley?' she wonders. Perhaps. She even finds the @ sign in the name rather quaint. It reminds her of the time at the beginning of the 2000s when the dotcom companies were booming. 'The @ was really cool, and I love the fact that it will stay in the name, an everlasting anachronism.' Marina also says she loves the place, the quiet streets, the spring sunshine, breaks from work, the broad streets. 'It's much nicer working here than anywhere else.'

The initial idea behind the scheme was all to do with dedicating a district to technology and innovation, to the point that some business premises that did not comply with this requirement had to be replaced. Ultra-Local Records, for example, a shop selling fanzines and vinyl located on Carrer de Pujades, had to negotiate a number of obstacles to be allowed to set up shop. Raül Chamorro, one of those who runs the concern, says that when he applied for a licence he was told that his business had nothing to do with innovation and so it was impossible. Chamorro wondered, 'What's the problem? It's just a shop.' He was finally able to take advantage of a loophole to open up, however. How? His shop is based in an old residential building and not in a warehouse or office building. The shop has been in existence since 2012, organises concerts and has regular customers, but the main reason it is still there is because the owner of the premises has resisted constant pressure from the property-management company to increase the rent. You feel as if you are treading on ground that costs a lot of money, that it costs more with each passing minute and that it could, in fact, cost a lot more. A perfect city plan in which the only things surplus to requirements are people.

Mansilla stresses that Barcelona's connection with tourism is deeply entrenched in the city, having been heavily promoted both by socialist and conservative Catalan governments. Slogans such as 'Barcelona, make yourself beautiful' or accolades such as 'Barcelona, the best shop in the world' have much to do with that post-Olympics Barcelona and its slavish devotion to tourism and business interests, always ready to flaunt the best version of itself to the outside world. District 22@ is a part of that philosophy of a modern Barcelona open to everyone. There is one worrying fact, though: Barcelona's first strategic plan for tourism appeared in 2005 and the second in 2017, when Ada Colau was elected mayor. 'Up until then tourism had been regulating itself,' says Mansilla.

'District 22@ has already been around for a long time, but it's only now that it's become physically aggressive,' says Chamorro. Carmen Baqués, his business partner in the shop, uses different words to describe the splendour of the skyscrapers. 'The shape of the buildings isn't on a human level. It's a neighbourhood for office buildings, not for people'. They hear about shops or associations closing down every month, the now defunct residents' association Fundició de Poblenou being one. Rent hikes or the acquisition of a building by an investment fund result in many associations having to find somewhere else outside the neighbourhood, which, in practice, means they disappear.

The 2008 financial crisis led to the initial aims of the plan (inspired by tech industry models in the USA) being amended and allowing types of businesses to open that were not originally in the brief. So the hotels (*many* hotels) and call centres arrived. There are also some people who never left: the top floor of the Encants Market offers a panoramic view of a settlement of around two hundred migrants living in shacks they built themselves. Mansilla says that repeated attempts have been made, with varying degrees of success, to 'clean up the city' by removing signs of poverty, keeping them out of sight or shifting them elsewhere. However, urban conflict, which is fundamentally a battle for space and the different uses made of that space, is still alive and kicking. On several occasions I have tried to talk to some of the men who deal in scrap metal. It's impossible, and each time I try I feel upset, I feel pathetic, too white and hostile. Only Yunus, a forty-year-old Senegalese man, stops to tell me that he doesn't want to appear in a story because he's undocumented and a lot of people are racist.

When it comes down to it the residents are mainly reproaching the institutions for selling off the neighbourhood to vulture funds and corporate lobbies. 'Everything looks great, and it's all well lit, but who's it for, what's it for?' says

Aurora Pelegrí, a 63-year-old who's lived in the neighbourhood all her life. She is not against the improvements or the radical changes made over the past twenty years, and neither is she nostalgic about times past. She remembers her mother's stories about the area's industrial days and tells me that when she was little 'there was smoke belching out everywhere, everything was filthy and dusty, and when you went to the beach you came home covered in tar'.

At the end of the 19th century Poblenou had the highest number of industrial units in Spain and was even referred to as the Catalan Manchester. Its proximity to the sea, the low price of land and an abundance of water made it an attractive place for different types of factories – textile factories in particular but also flour mills and many smaller workshops and warehouses. The process of deindustrialisation began in the mid-1960s, and a large number of sites were left vacant. Pelegrí condemns the fact that for decades this working-class neighbourhood was neglected and simply left to decline. Some of the largest shanty towns in the city were built in this area during the 20th century, including Somorrostro, Pequín and Transcementiri. 'But as for what's happening now ...' Pelegrí suddenly stops, right in the middle of the street – a dramatic pause. 'What's happening now, I don't know where it's going to end. What use is a neighbourhood with no parks?' She tells me that she sent a letter to the council a few days ago requesting that a park be built nearby as she was tired of having to walk so far just to be able to play with her granddaughters. 'We're beginning to be surrounded by office buildings and hotels. There's nothing else here,' says a man walking past as I'm talking to Aurora, and he points out all the building

That was the name given to Poblenou, the coastal neighbourhood to the northeast of the centre of Barcelona, in San Martí, the 'Smokestack District'. The concentration of factories was extremely high, with 40 per cent of Catalonia's cotton industry being based there. Today the area has radically changed its appearance, although some vestiges of its industrial, working-class past survive: one example that really stands out is the Flor de Maig cooperative, founded by workers in 1890 and still operating as a people's school and university. Poblenou was a stronghold of the workers' movement, where people tried to club together to deal with poverty and degradation; this they did by buying basic goods in bulk and selling them locally at low prices and by helping the most disadvantaged and the sick as well as providing everyone with places to gather, including educational establishments. Literacy classes were organised, along with Esperanto lessons, chess tournaments and musical evenings. Some cooperatives even began to mint coins, known as *patacons*, for trade between fellow members. But, above all, they provided funds for strikers so they could sustain themselves while picketing, thus providing support for workers' struggles. And yet, in spite of the solidarity between its inhabitants, Poblenou remained an insalubrious neighbourhood, hit by epidemics of typhus, cholera and dengue fever. There were even shanty towns up until the second half of the 20th century, a recent history that the city of Barcelona tried to gloss over and which has only more recently become part of its collective memory.

Metal and wrought iron ready to be sold to the scrap dealers in Poblenou, where the price is €0.06/kilo.

sites around us. Aurora calls for 'more social housing and more homes. That's all we need. The neighbourhood is very nice, that's the truth, and I'm not against the superblocks.'

This is a common opinion. Many Poblenou residents stress that the neighbourhood is definitely better than it was a few decades ago, that it's pleasant to walk around and see the new green spaces. 'There's no comparison with what was here before.' The only problem is the inevitability that these improvements will bring with them an increase in property prices and some current residents being replaced by those with higher incomes, a classic process of speculation and gentrification. There is nothing unique about

this; it is the reality in many cities in the context of global capitalism.

Albert València is a 25-year-old architect and an activist in Poblenou. I came across him through a documentary called *Gent del Barri*, in which he conducts a kind of political 'free tour'. In the video he explains the case of Passatge Morenes. It is a prime example that helps us understand the property aggression that's going on here. This narrow street, with its low-rise houses, is one of those surrounded by twelve-storey office buildings. The residents here were due to be pushed out after their street was 'affected' by the plan. One woman tells me that it is ironic that the residents are *affected* by city planning. It turns out that the property owner bought up 60 per cent of the block, and in this case had the power to change its use. All these houses, says València in the video, were to be demolished. The residents finally managed to win the right to stay through sheer pressure. However, the surrounding area is still being transformed, bordered by large hotels and the promise of more office buildings.

'You can't create something artificially. Cities and the texture of neighbourhoods aren't created just by placing a green space there. That's why there are green spaces and parks here that aren't used because no one lives nearby. There are also places that are losing neighbourhood life,' says Baqués, the woman from the record shop. It reminds her of the Olympic Village in the Sant Martí district, which was like a ghost town before it underwent radical change along with Poblenou in preparation for the 1992 Olympic Games. Chamorro also makes an interesting comment: many of the people who come to work here don't take part in any activities in the neighbourhood, as many of the companies or co-working companies encourage a type of after-work leisure activity that takes place on their own rooftops or in specific places. In a way, they are isolated communities that are just passing through, living something like 'the *Barcelona experience*, good weather, the beach, working in the office or from home, all that' for a while but not much more. In some way, perhaps, it is the post-industrial corporate evolution of the 'typical' Spanish package of paella, sun and flamenco. On the subject of these white-collar workers, the anthropologist Mansilla explains that, although there is great disparity in salaries and perhaps they are above the national average, they cannot be compared with salaries offered by technology companies in other countries in northern Europe or the USA, so 'perhaps we are becoming a refuge for cheap labour for the technology companies, or Europe's call centre'.

'They would like the city to be the apotheosis of what is organic, meaningful, settled, coagulated, crystallised, stratified, subjectivised ... That's why they think about the city in terms of plans, maps, projects. By contrast, by definition, what is urban amounts to the inorganic, the non-meaningful, the disjointed, the disorganised ... a body with just bones, just skin, an entity that only knows and is aware of the strength of whatever it is that shakes it or crosses it in all directions,' states Manuel Delgado, who is also an anthropologist and understands the urban model of the city well, in 'Lo Urbano Como Texto Ilegible y Cuerpo Sin Órganos' ('The Urban as an Illegible Text and a Body Without Organs', *Crítica Urbana*, July 2020).

In 2017, within the framework of an exhibition called *Malas Calles* ('Bad Streets') at the Virreina Centre de la Imatge, the documentary *La Lucha por el Espacio Urbano* ('The Fight for Urban Space') by Jacobo Sucari listed some of the Poblenou residents' protests against the expansion of 22@ newbuilds and in favour of saving Can Ricart, an old factory declared as an asset of national interest but which has today fallen into disuse through bad management. Some of the businesses in Can Ricart were evicted as were some other squatted premises, as they were not 'in line' with the innovation macro-project. As yet no real use has been found for the old factory, and it remains in a kind of limbo. The Poblenou residents who managed to save the structure are critical of its neglect, and in 2020 some demanded that the city council take it over. Today Can Ricart is a kind of oasis – albeit one that is dilapidated and underused.

As I walk along, I think that its very emptiness can be seen as a kind of resistance. On a working day the old courtyard in that industrial complex is a haven of tranquillity, a long way from the JCBs and noise of machinery; this space seems to sing the praises of relaxation and taking things easy. One day I bump into a girl calmly eating lentils out of a plastic container as she's looking at her phone. She tells me she doesn't want to go back to work. Another day I creep past a workman stretched out on a bench having a wonderful siesta. I think that this is not a fight between tradition and progress – that's not the dilemma – it is simply a matter of remembering that spaces and their uses cannot depend exclusively on whichever investor happens to be in the ascendant. In this area I believe that most people are not against new ways of working, nor are they against the technology companies. Perhaps it's simply a case of treating the residents fairly, decently and with understanding.

District 22@ was also originally much more progressive than other projects implemented in other areas of the city that have also suffered from decline through property speculation and gentrification. Certain minimum standards were laid down, such as preserving the industrial heritage, which is why it is not uncommon to see works chimneys or the remains of factories from the last century. Regulations relating to areas of public and protected housing were also brought in. But in twenty years only 1,600 units of social housing have been built, 40 per cent of the number planned initially. It is a fact that Spain has the lowest levels of social housing in Europe.

'Flirting at work, which is the only legitimate thing an office is good for, takes place in this filthy environment. It's not easy falling in love or touching each other's faces because you always end up getting tainted and messing everything up, and, even though you really try, you always end up thinking that *you're better off not liking anyone at work*. The middle managers are swimming in shit and outrageously put

their feet in it by offering free apples as if they are doing you a favour. I'd rather eat shit than that free apple, I hear an employee say.' That's the dystopian vision I uploaded to my Instagram feed. I think about it now as I'm walking through a co-working space with the windows open and through which I can see an enormous bowl, not just with free apples but with a *selection* of fruit. It's one of those spaces with enormous sofas and large tables where the employees seem to have been taken out of a free-image bank. On one of my trips I pass a building with a sign above the door displaying WeWork. It occurs to me how absurd it must be to go into the office each day to a place that tells you 'we work'.

The spaces located in the superblocks with community picnic tables, large tables with chairs, these all fill up with workers at lunchtime. There is also La Gran Clariana, a green space with public deckchairs where you can relax. One sunny morning I realise that these places are spaces where, at least during their break, people are different. It is something of an anomaly to eat in the open air in the city without having to pay or being able to relax in a deckchair for free without being on the beach. I think perhaps that's what makes District 22@ come alive and at the same time makes it feel odd. Mundane activities (eating, sleeping) turn into a kind of exception that is visible to everyone.

When night falls the area is lit up by all the lights left on in the office buildings. I think about Baqués again, who was on the point of starting a campaign to turn the lights off. As I walk away, most of the noise from the building sites has stopped, and I pass more vacant plots. If I try to imagine what 22@ will be like in twenty years' time, it feels there is still something unpredictable about it all. 🐦

Cities and Names

MARINA ESPASA

Translated by Tiago Miller

There's an invisible line that joins Sarrià, a small well-to-do neighbourhood at the foot of Barcelona's northern hills, with La Verneda, a working-class neighbourhood close to the sea and the river Besòs, full of high-rise flats built during the Franco dictatorship. Crossing Barcelona from north-west to south-east, like a tightrope walker on a high wire, the ghost of the Colombian writer Gabriel García Márquez could follow the same route. He'd fly out of the window of his small apartment on Carrer Caponata – where, in the 1960s, literary agent Carmen Balcells set him up so he'd have a place to write – eventually arriving at the corner of Concili de Trento and Treball to admire the imposing wood-and-glass building there that appears to be made of folded paper, almost like an origami sculpture. But his city crossing would take him fifty-five years, because it wouldn't be until 2022 when this brand-new cultural centre would open its doors in a neighbourhood hardly blessed with an overabundance of such places. He'd read his name next to the word 'Library', along with a couple of lines taken from his autobiography, *Living to Tell the Tale* – 'Life is not what one lived but what one remembers, and how one remembers it in order to recount it' – and he'd think to himself how he'd retain a vivid memory of that day, as bright and agile as a lizard slipping between two rocks.

Let's say he arrives on Saturday 28 May 2022. He'd find hundreds of people outside – everyone from curious passers-by to local residents to state representatives (even the mayor!) – live music, traditional Catalan and Colombian dancers, storytellers, a copper bust of Márquez himself, comfortable sofas, flights of stairs, magazine areas, a studio with the

MARINA ESPASA is the author of the novels *La Dona Que Es Va Perdre* (Labutxaca, 2012) and *El Dia del Cérvol* (L'Altra Editorial, 2016) as well as being a literary critic for the daily *Ara* and a translator. She has worked as a cultural journalist on TV book shows and, from 2016 to 2019, was responsible for the initiative Barcelona, UNESCO City of Literature. Since 2021 she has been involved in the literary programme of Finestres, the Barcelona bookshop of which she is co-founder.

name Radio Macondo, an events space, a corner with the *Mortadelo y Filemón* comics that Catalan and Spanish children have enjoyed since the late 1950s, when Francisco Ibáñez, a resident of the Barcelona district of La Verneda, came up with the idea of following the misadventures of a pair of absent-minded secret agents. There'd even be a hammock crying out for someone to stretch out in it with a book. He'd go up and down the wooden stairs and in and out of the children's area, magazine corner and events room like someone entering and exiting a forest, with naturalness and vigour, without knowing exactly where he was or when he'd fully emerge again.

He'd soon find a corner displaying all of his books, an extensive list of novels and non-fiction capped by *One Hundred Years of Solitude*, one of the most ubiquitous books in the homes of the progressive Barcelona bourgeoisie of the 1970s and 1980s. He'd be amazed by the technological advances of the future: computers, a radio studio, lifts, self-service machines for borrowing books ... Sitting in front of one of the computers, he'd magically know how to work the mouse, and, after a quick Google search, he'd be made aware that there were forty public libraries on a par with that one in Barcelona's vast network, designed to nourish spirits (and satisfy many material needs) across the city. These are spaces that are the first contact with books for a large number of children who don't have any at home, a point of reference for migrants so they can do just what he is doing – sit at a computer to browse the internet, ask questions or send emails to the loved ones they had to leave on the other side of the world – and a morning meeting place for the elderly to read the newspaper or university students who need silence and somewhere to concentrate before exams. Forty

centres to find oxygen, refuge or simply a friendly face. Hundreds of thousands of books changing hands between more than half a million library users each and every year. On that particular May morning more than a thousand library cards were issued to local residents, joining the more than one million Barcelonans who already had one.

If he finds himself dizzy and disorientated by such numbers, he might decide to go for a stroll outside the library, whereupon he'd discover a beautiful row of pine trees (an alien presence among the high-rise blocks), bars emitting the homely aroma of fried food and the Rambla de Guipúscoa, home to commerce and life like any other *rambla* in the city. But soon he'd spy a disconcerting modern building with ominously dark windows in front of which flies an oversized Spanish flag. Any passer-by would be able to inform him that it is La Verneda police station, known for its 'foreigners' department – in other words, where migrants lacking official documents (like him) find themselves before being deported, imprisoned or sent to the purgatory of a detention centre. A place where interrogation is synonymous with intimidation and, even when inmates aren't harassed and harmed, they are certainly treated without the respect and humanity they deserve. A library behind a police station has to offset a lot of negative energy, thinks the ghost of García Márquez, as a bead of sweat runs down his forehead.

Tired of playing the tightrope walker, and depressed by a neighbourhood where one of the gates of hell is located, he'd head underground and take the metro back up to Sarrià: purple line, change for the red line, then a local train. When he gets off he'll feel as if he's alighted in another world, for the old village of Sarrià,

annexed to Barcelona in 1921, is a quiet refuge of peaceful streets with quaint houses and the odd apartment block. The latter, however, are of a different order here, nowhere near as monolithic and drab, and many have a private garden and secluded swimming pool. He remembers that he has to pass by the stationery shop to buy another box of paper so the click-clack of his typewriter doesn't fall unnecessarily silent. But no one said time travel was an easy endeavour, and it would no longer be 1968 but still 2022, and Senyora Balcells wouldn't pick up the telephone to solve for him the problems of where to eat that evening or to suggest a place to spend a couple of relaxing weeks by the sea. The stationery shop below his home would no longer be there either. However, the key would still open the door to the apartment, but inside there'd be another man, an insurance broker who'd decided to have lunch at home after a couple of his calls were cancelled. The shock would be mutual. Nephew to the president of the apartment-block's residents' committee,

the insurance broker wouldn't think twice about sending his uncle a WhatsApp to warn him of an individual with a moustache like that of the famous Colombian writer trying to repossess the flat, which evidently wasn't his. The ghost would inevitably maintain his sense of decorum and decency by turning around and heading back down the stairs. Afterwards he'd seek refuge in the metro and make his way directly to La Verneda.

The insurance broker's uncle, a venerable ex-banker of eighty-seven, would furrow his brow while reading his nephew's slightly alarming message. It must have something to do with the impertinent phone calls he'd been receiving from some pen pusher at the town hall who was requesting permission to install a plaque on the front of the building to commemorate the fact that the writer Gabriel García Márquez had once lived there. (The author of *One Hundred Years of Solitude*, yeah, yeah, sure, he knows about Márquez. As a young man Márquez had been required reading for any wannabe leftie liberal, but that sort of thing isn't so fashionable now. Am I right?) A circular blue plaque (*blue*, of all colours!) smack in the middle of the façade – a genuine assault on good taste, if ever there was one! Did they seriously believe he'd allow his home to be turned into a magnet for tourists, phones in one hand and bottles of water in the other? Not a chance. He knows the rules and regulations of those committee meetings by heart; he knows that a single 'nay' would be enough to block any initiative that involved modifying a building's façade. What's more, he is the president (each time he says that word to himself he makes an almost imperceptible movement of his shoulders that denotes both pride and satisfaction); in other words, he'll clip the wings of that little birdie. Let's be clear. There is no place for any so-called cultural initiatives dictated by public authorities in this neighbourhood or on this building. What would be next? Telling them to leave coffee and cakes on the doorstep to feed the oxymoron that is 'cultural tourism'? And, to top it all, there's this nonsense

about a man dressed as García Márquez attempting to repossess the very flat that he gave to his nephew years ago. What a ludicrous story! Sure, the world was going mad, but this really was taking liberties.

Strolling along Rambla de Guipúscoa, the ghost of García Márquez notices some inscriptions on the central divide engraved on stainless-steel panels. The words commemorate historic events that took place in Sant Martí de Provençals, another town annexed to Barcelona towards the end of the 19th century, not long before Sarrià: shootings, uprisings, popular festivals. These are the work of Francesc Torres, a Barcelona-born artist who lived and worked for decades in the Big Apple. Letters running along the *rambla*, letters on a library façade, the pristine wall of an apartment building; homes and objects aren't always given a name.

Before arriving at the police station he turns on to Concili de Trento and is once again in front of the library steps, still covered in confetti after the ceremony. He senses that end-of-a-party feeling; the bars nearby are full of people drinking beer in celebration of who knows what, bright smiles on their lips, like the last round of champagne and good wishes on New Year's Eve. Two old women carry a child's buggy down the library steps saying, 'If taxes were always spent on things like this then they'd be worth paying.' Meanwhile the librarians are switching off the computers and lights and breathing sighs of relief after what's been one of the most intense days of their working lives.

Without being seen, the ghost goes up to the second floor, browses a few shelves, before stretching out on the hammock with a book in his hands. Surely it's impossible to imagine a better place than this to begin reading Gabriel García Márquez's memoirs.

An Author Recommends

Two films, a singer and
a book to understand
Barcelona, chosen by:

POLA OLOIXARAC
Translated by Kit Maude

FILMS
VICKY CRISTINA BARCELONA
Woody Allen
2008
ALL ABOUT MY MOTHER
Pedro Almodóvar
1999

Haughty, elegant and reserved, I've always preferred to view Barcelona through the eyes of foreigners, and, although the eponymous movie *Barcelona* (Whit Stillman, 1994) ranks high on my personal list, I think that *Vicky Cristina Barcelona* (Woody Allen, 2008) unwittingly captures something essential about the city. It's right there in the title: Barcelona is one of the girls in a trio looking for true love, the kind of love that embraces and saves you. *Vicky Cristina Barcelona* portrays a world of upper-class artists from Barcelona. Javier Bardem plays an intense, virile painter who believes only in sensuality and his art. He lives in a mansion in Pedralbes, one of Barcelona's most exclusive neighbourhoods, and is trapped in a turbulent affair with another painter, Penélope Cruz. They love each other so much that they can't stand the sight of each other, and so they invite Scarlett Johansson, who resembles a young Marilyn Monroe in a vest, to join

them in an amorous threesome. In order to love one another, the residents of Barcelona need a third party, a witness – tourists. The romantic pact with tourism is what keeps the passions that writhe in Barcelona's soul in check, although their true obsession might well be their penchant for loving/quarrelling with other Catalans. Barcelona's self-love needs the blushing foreigner in order to flourish, making us immigrants, a little like Scarlett: fascinated by the city's intense beauty without really getting what it's actually all about, a bind from which the blonde eventually manages to extricate herself.

Another blonde who is able to make her escape is Cecilia Roth in *All About My Mother* (Pedro Almodóvar, 1999), until she returns to Barcelona to settle some unfinished business. A contemporary melodrama in which the femme fatale is a trans woman who has seduced and impregnated two women, the only thing that can't be forgiven in this film is the fact she ran away. 'Only unfulfilled love can be romantic,' says Penélope Cruz in *Vicky Cristina Barcelona*, while in *All About My Mother* she plays a pregnant nun. Like Gaudí's Sagrada Família, Barcelona reaches for the heavens, revelling in its unfinished, constantly transforming state.

THE SINGER
ARCA

Arca is the latest name adopted by the formidable artist Alejandra Ghersi. Born in a male body in Caracas, Venezuela, Alejandra trained as a music producer in the USA before eventually settling in Barcelona and becoming a smouldering woman artist. Creator of a potent, sinuous electronic sound, Arca is like a Barcelona Grimes but darker and more mysterious, a kind of Lady Gaga with a dark, 90s sensibility (her influences include the animated sci-fi series *Æon Flux* and the band Nine Inch Nails). Arca uses fashion as a shiny suit of artistic armour in which she seems to perceive herself not as a woman but rather as a new species from the future, one that is in permanent flux, with her music's overpowering beat at her core. Arca has worked with Björk and Rosalía (another superdiva from Barcelona), and I believe that an important feature of her music is an introspective journey, an electronic spiral that takes in both trap and reggaeton in a shifting, transformative flow, a mutating mixture that ends up sounding like lullabies for a majestic alien sizing the world up before swallowing it whole.

The Barcelona tradition is grounded in the satirical picaresque, with *City of Wonders* by Eduardo Mendoza taking pride of place at the summit of the literary Pyrenees of Catalonia and *Vida Privada* ('Private Life') by Josep Maria de Sagarra providing the base rock. However, I believe that the book that best captures Barcelona's spirit today is *Corona de Flores* ('Crown of Flowers') by Javier Calvo, in which the city, with all its pride and intrigue, is seen through a hair-raisingly freaky lens. Calvo's Barcelona is populated by Gothic creatures, murderous phrenologists, shady anatomists experimenting on corpses and decadent novelists who dream of establishing a new morality. The passion of the prose is overwhelming, the supernatural does its ghoulish dance and Barcelona looms with a medieval air over its weird residents and blind alleys. This bibliophilic novel is, in fact, far more realistic than Mendoza's harmonious fresco. For me, it presents the madness of the city in a new light: when I go to El Raval I can feel his Gothic characters all around me, bent over arcane volumes as they mix their crazy potions. Even the city's recent, cooler vibe feels sinister to me: *come closer, your perdition is here*. Against this backdrop Calvo, the odd one out in the family, gleams as dark and bright as obsidian.

POLA OLOIXARAC is a Barcelona-based Argentinian writer. Her 2008 debut novel *Las Teorías Salvajes*, published in English as *Savage Theories* (Soho Press, 2017), was a bestseller in Argentina and many other countries. In 2010 Granta included her in their list of best young Spanish-speaking writers. She has contributed to *The New York Times*, *El País* and writes regularly for *La Nación*. Her latest novel, published in Spanish in 2019, is *Mona* (Farrar, Straus and Giroux, 2021, USA / Serpent's Tail, UK, 2022).

The Playlist

SERGIO CABALLERO
Translated by Kit Maude

You can listen to this playlist at:
open.spotify.com/user/iperborea

These twelve tracks chart the story of one of the most exciting revolutions to take place in the Barcelona music scene in recent times. All were written within the last seven years by artists under the age of thirty, some of the creative forces behind the recent explosion Barcelona has witnessed in genres such as trap, dancehall and reggaeton. But, more than that, they represent a radical shift in how the music industry works and promotes its talents.

These young artists have turned their backs on the old models and done away with formalities. Their music is created in bedrooms and home studios, they sing to their audiences without striving for perfection, using playback and Auto-Tune and making their performances a party for their peers. They release their work and find fame directly on YouTube and social networks, including Instagram and, more recently, TikTok, rejecting the macro-structures of the music industry and refusing to seek out record labels, making the suits come knocking at *their* doors instead.

This movement has produced such global phenomena as Rosalía, street idols like Cecilio G and Morad, emo anti-icons like Rojuu, sought-after producers like Steve Lean and El Guincho and songwriters like Kaydy Cain, Yung Beef, Khaled and La Zowi – who pioneered PXXR GVNG, one of the first trap groups in Spain.

These twelve artists are behind a radical shift in the status quo and the arrival of a new era in music, and they represent a scene with a punk personality that has broken the mould for creating, distributing and performing music.

SERGIO CABALLERO is a co-founder and co-director of the Sónar Music Festival, and from the outset he has been the festival's art director. As an artist he moves between electronic music, visual arts and film directing. His film *Finisterrae* (2010) won the Tiger Award at the Rotterdam Film Festival, after which he made *Ancha Es Castilla / N'Importe Quoi* (2014) and *Je Te Tiens* (2019), which was presented at the Cannes Film Festival.

1

La Zowi,
Zora Jones
Obra de Arte
2016

2

Aleesha,
Emilia
828
2022

3

Cecilio G.,
Limabeatz
Pikete Espacial
2018

4

Kinder Malo,
Pimp Flaco
<3
2017

5

Bizarrap,
Morad
*Morad: Bzrp
Music Sessions*
2021

6

Bad Gyal
*Nueva York
(Tot*)*
2021

7

Rosalía
Aute Cuture
2019

8

Beny Jr,
El Guincho
Combo la L
2021

9

Juicy BAE,
PMP
Xq Tan Difícil
2022

10

Leïti Sene,
iseekarlo
Bitcoin
2022

11

PXXR GVNG
Cigala
2015

12

Rojuu, fox1
Internet
2022

Digging Deeper

FICTION

Javier Calvo
Wonderful World
Harper Perennial, 2010

Javier Cercas
Even the Darkest Night
Alfred A. Knopf, 2022, USA
/ MacLehose, UK, 2022

Rupert Thomson
Barcelona Dreaming
Other Press, 2021, USA
/ Corsair, 2022, UK

Helen Constantine (ed.)
Barcelona Tales
Oxford University Press, 2019

Mathias Énard
Street of Thieves
Fitzcarraldo, 2015

Ildefonso Falcones
The Cathedral of the Sea
Black Swan, 2009

Alicia Giménez-Bartlett
The Petra Delicado Mysteries (Series)
Europa Editions

Carmen Laforet
Nada
Modern Library, 2008, USA
/ Vintage, 2020, UK

Juan Marsé
The Calligraphy of Dreams
MacLehose, 2014

Esteban Martín
The Gaudi Key
William Morrow, 2008

Eduardo Mendoza
City of Wonders
MacLehose, 2022

Albert Sánchez Piñol
Victus: The Fall of Barcelona
Harper, 2014

Pablo Tusset
*The Best Thing that Can
Happen to a Croissant*
Canongate, 2005

Manuel Vázquez Montalbán
The Pepe Carvalho Investigations (Series)
Melville House

Enrique Vila-Matas
Mac and His Problem
Vintage, 2019, USA / Harvill Secker, 2019, UK

NON-FICTION

Barcelona en Comú, Debbie Bookchin
and Ada Colau
*Fearless Cities: A Guide to the
Global Municipalist Movement*
New Internationalist, 2019

Helena Buffery and Carlota Caulfield (eds)
Barcelona: Visual Culture, Space and Power
University of Wales Press, 2012

Andrew Dowling
Catalonia: A New History
Routledge, 2022

Michael Eude
A People's History of Catalonia
Pluto, 2022

Simon Kuper
*Barça: The Rise and Fall of the Club
that Built Modern Football*
Short Books, 2022

Gary McDonogh and Sergi Martinez-Rigol
Barcelona
Polity, 2019

Raphael Minder
*The Struggle for Catalonia:
Rebel Politics in Spain*
Hurst, 2017

Jordi Puntí
Messi: Lessons in Style
Short Books, 2019

Rainer Zerbst
Gaudí: The Complete Works
Taschen, 2020

ARTICLES

Stephen Burgen and Paola de Grenet
'How Tourism Is Killing
Barcelona: A Photo Essay'
Guardian, 30 August 2018

Nando Cruz
'Primavera Sound, el Cortijo del Indie'
El Confidencial, 1 June 2016

Rebecca Mead
'The Airbnb Invasion of Barcelona'
The New Yorker, 22 April 2019

David Roberts
'Barcelona's Radical Plan to Take
Back Streets from Cars'
Vox, 26 May 2019

Michael Stothard
'Barcelona: Espionage, Secret Police
and the Battle for Catalonia'
Financial Times, 20 June 2018

Manel Vidal Boix
'Messi, l'Heroi Automàtic'
Catalunyadiari, 23 August 2021

Graphic design and art direction:
Tomo Tomo and Pietro Buffa

Photography: Marc Gómez del Moral
Photographic content curated by Prospekt Photographers

Illustrations: Edoardo Massa

Infographics and cartography: Pietro Buffa

Managing editor (English-language edition): Simon Smith

Thanks to: Miguel Aguilar, Simone Bertelegni, Cristina Casaburi,
Camila Enrich, Patricia Escalona, Marc Gómez del Moral,
Marcela Hattemer, Victor Hurtado, Maria Lynch, Claudia Mallart,
Jan Martí, Marina Penalva, Cecilia Ricciarelli, Ella Sher,
Luis Solano, Txell Torrent

The opinions expressed in this publication are those of the authors
and do not purport to reflect the views and opinions
of the publishers. All content not specifically credited was written
by *The Passenger*.

http://europaeditions.com/thepassenger
http://europaeditions.co.uk/thepassenger
#ThePassengerMag

The Passenger – Barcelona
© Iperborea S.r.l., Milan, and Europa Editions, 2023

Translators: Catalan – Tiago Miller; Italian – Alan Thawley;
Spanish – Simon Deefholts ('The Art of Observing Bridges from
Below', 'The Mapping of Paradise', 'Barcelona, Festival City'),
Kit Maude ('Get Out There and Enjoy Yourselves', 'An Author
Recommends', 'The Playlist'), Kathryn Phillips-Miles ('Superblock
503', 'El Raval: The Capital of a Country That Doesn't Exist',
'The Sea and Me: A Conversation on Wheels', 'Offices to Let')

Translations © Iperborea S.r.l., Milan, and Europa Editions, 2023

ISBN 9781787704374

Printed on Munken Pure thanks to the support of Arctic Paper

Printed by ELCOGRAF S.p.A., Verona, Italy